Coping in the Country

Clear Creek Press
Box 35
Rough & Ready, CA 95975

Slightly different versions of many of these pieces were originally published 1991 - 1996 through the Clear Creek Features Syndicate in several California newspapers including the Valley Voice, Grass Valley Union, Auburn Sentinel, Mariposa Gazette, Placerville Mountain Democrat, Rabbit Creek Journal, Tule River Times, and Sacramento Bee.

Library of Congress Cataloging-in-Publication Data

Drummond, Mike.
    Coping in the Country.

    1. Humor - Country Living - Essays - Satire

ISBN 1-889586-00-5

Illustrations by Peter Adams
Cover Design: LeeAnn Brook Design
Cover Illustration: copyright Wallace Tripp.
    Used with permission, all rights reserved.

Clear Creek Press
Box 35
Rough & Ready CA 95975

To Anna, With Love

ACKNOWLEDGEMENTS

Many thanks to Linda Whitmore, erstwhile editor of the equally erstwhile Valley Voice, where most of these pieces first appeared.

Thanks too, to the folks at BackHome Magazine on whose BackPorch I've camped so amiably for the past few years.

And special thanks to Anna, my wife and best friend.

CONTENTS

My Fortress of Solitude

When I felt like getting away from it all I used to hike up to a small granite outcropping high on a hill here at Clear Creek Ranch. On a good day I could see the mauve outline of the Coast Range mountains far to the west. On stormy days I could watch the weather fronts approach. But no matter the weather, it was a wonderful retreat, a place for quiet contemplation.

At first I stood, or squatted on my heels, or sat directly on the cold, hard stone. But soon the lazy side of my rather decadent nature took over. I brought a little plastic-covered cushion to pad my otherwise uninsulated backside, and after dutifully carting it back and forth on several occasions, I left it there. It was hidden from view from the ranch house perspective, unless you were a buzzard or a redtail hawk soaring overhead.

Eventually the cushion cracked, the victim of broiling sun and freezing winters. I replaced it with a low-slung tubular aluminum beach chair covered in plastic webbing. And soon after, I attached a little umbrella onto the chair to shield my balding noggin from the harmful UV rays bouncing my way.

There were times when my wife would use this retreat too. And times when we went up there together. But there was only one chair and really no level space for a second. On those occasions, while my wife rested in the chair, I stood about chivalrously rather than risk sitting shiver-ously on the ice-cold stone.

The idea of a bench large enough to accommodate both of us was discussed, but the rounded nature of the rock provided a problem. Unless I could build a small platform to support it. The prospect seemed daunting, but not impossible. Over the next several months I lugged lumber, dug footings, and pounded nails.

The result was a sturdy 12'x12' redwood deck, warm enough to sit upon with legs dangling over the side, and certainly roomy enough for the wrought iron and wood park bench we hauled up there in pieces and reassembled.

The little umbrella seemed inadequate now and we talked of a larger canopy to shade us. I erected posts and cross beams and rigged up a shade cloth cover. This was fine in the summer, but it provided little shelter during the rainy season. That autumn I added a peaked roof, shingled in such a way that it blended in with its natural surroundings.

At times we slept up there in the open air, not quite under the stars, and we felt we needed a dependable light source. Our Coleman lantern hissed too much, and an oil lamp seemed dangerous. I strung together some heavy duty extension cords and although it was a bit of an eyesore snaking its way up the hillside, we were able to power a small table lamp. I dragged a small table up there to set it on, right next to the roll-away double bed.

One unforseen side effect of a light bulb shining in the middle of nowhere is bugs. They found it fascinating and thronged around, even when we switched to one of those yellow "bug lights." Insect repellant worked against the mosquitos, but it did nothing to keep bulb-scorched moths from flying into our faces. Screens were the answer. And, of course a screen door. And then some glass for the two windward sides so the view wouldn't be obstructed, and sudden gusts wouldn't blow our blankets off.

And that was all, until the night I had to wait down at the house for an important phone call. I barked my shins stumbling up the trail in the dark. We needed a phone line up there. Telephone poles were out of the question aesthetically, so we rented some ditching equipment and dug a trench. Two actually, one for the phone and power lines, and another for a water

pipe. You see, sometimes my wife likes to have a drink of water in the middle of the night.

That winter we replaced the screen walls with cedar siding and insulation, and with the help of two friends hauled a little woodstove up there. And we put down carpeting to cover the original redwood deck.

Now it's hard to get into a proper meditative state up there, what with the phone ringing and the water faucet dripping. So the other day when I wanted some solitude, I climbed up on the roof. The view is still great. And from that new vantage point I noticed a little rock outcropping nearby, so obscured by brush that I'd never seen it before.

Tomorrow I plan to go over for a closer look, maybe take an old cushion to sit on. You know, one that I can leave there.

A Little Bat Room Humor

One evening my wife mentioned that the bats weren't flying around our yard eating insects like they once did; and wouldn't it be nice if I built a bat house like the one she had clipped out of a magazine.

When I agreed without argument, she eyed me suspiciously.

Naturally, my first order of business was to fire off a mail order for more power tools. As a veteran home handyman, I knew if I had the right tool for the job, anything was possible. I also found it a lot easier to hand that "right tool" to the repairman when he arrived to un-do my initial handiwork.

A week later, the entire contents of several pages of the Sears tool catalog appeared on my doorstep. Now I was prepared to handle anything that required cutting, drilling, nailing, smoothing, or shaping wood. In theory, anyway, and providing nobody at the power company accidentally unplugged the frayed extension cord that serves our rural neighborhood.

I was adjusting the bright red suspenders that supported my new fifty pound tool belt when a booklet that came with the tools caught my eye: "What Every Novice Handyman Should Know."

Well I was no novice, but I picked it up, hoping there was a chapter entitled "Overcoming Spousal Power Tool Resistance." There wasn't. The book's author kept harping on things like planning, safety precautions, and reading directions. I didn't want to waste time on stuff like that!

I drove my sports car to the lumberyard to get some wood for my project. A burly lumberjack-type employee was lounging near a pile of sawdust when I arrived. He smiled at me and I noticed that he had about as many teeth left as he had fingers. Seven or eight of each, I think. I didn't want to stare, even though he was taking a good long look at my new suspenders and tool belt.

"I need some wood," I said forcefully.

"Can you be a little more specific, Chief?"

"Not really. Just wood. I need some regular wood."

"That's different from the unleaded kind, right?"

"Look, I'm building a bat house . . ."

"Quite a project, a <u>bath</u> house. Are you sure you don't mean a bath <u>room</u>?"

"No, no, a bat house for flying bats. You know . . ." And I began flapping my arms and baring my teeth, presumably looking like a 150 pound bat wearing a plaid shirt and fifty pound tool belt.

"You know sir," he said as he backed away, "I just spotted a whole stack of regular wood right over there."

I may have made a bat impression on him, but the construction itself went smoothly. If I ignore the times when some stray parts were accidentally glued or nailed to the workbench.

A bat house is kind of like a bird house, except there is no door and no floor. The floor is the door. The bats fly in the open bottom and fall asleep while they hang upside down by their rear claws.

I painted the bat abode to match our house and proudly mounted the thing up above our front door and under the eaves. It was a neighborhood conversation piece. Soon everyone was pointing at it and whispering to each other.

The thing I liked about the project was that it was simple. For example, bats don't need indoor plumbing. With the open floor arrangement they use a primitive gravity flow system for eliminating wastes: everything drops straight down. The porch, however, is quite a mess most mornings.

My wife insists that the instructions warned about that.

"Why won't men ever use directions?" she asked.

"But I did use them," I insisted.

And I did, several times . . . to wipe glue off my hands and to mop up paint spills.

Gardening
on
$500 a Day

One spring evening after dinner, I donned a stiff new pair of overalls and proclaimed that I was going "back to the land." I hungered to grow my own tomatoes and corn . . . and squash and potatoes and peas and beans and lettuce and one-each of almost everything else that was nicely photographed in the seed catalogs that spread across our dining room table. When we had lived in the city, there wasn't much room for a garden.

My speech was filled with excited references to gardenly things: compost, crop-rotation, beneficial insects, irrigation, well-rotted manure. I longed to hear the quaint folk songs of the migrant workers as they rested in the shade of the mulberry tree after a long day's work at harvest time. I may have been hyperventilating.

My wife was encouraging -- in a tentative sort of way.

"I will happily clean and cook and can and eat any thing you grow," she purred, "but I refuse to gaze upon vegetables in progress or decline."

How well she knew me. In tiny city-gardens past, grey corn stalk skeletons loomed at improbable angles over the brown curled leaves of who-remembered-what. Let's face it, I'm an idea man, and follow-through, if it includes garden clean-up, is low on my priority list. My gardens only look neat at 2:00 AM on a moonless night, or right after a heavy snowfall. So I scratched my plans for that level spot next to the house.

The only other sunny patch on our property was about 100 yards uphill from the house, and the only access was a narrow winding trail. There was no water on the site, so I made a financial commitment and purchased a half mile of PVC pipe, a holding tank, and an automated sprinkler system.

About the time all this was delivered, I realized that the entire garden was covered with a thin layer of hard clay top soil that was bonded together in a sort of mineral rigor mortis. And there were hundreds of huge granite boulders barely submerged beneath the surface. It took days of rototilling and four dump truck loads of turkey manure, carted up the hill, one wheelbarrow at a time, to get the soil ready.

It was then I discovered I had built my garden at the animal kingdom crossroads. Every day there were fresh slither marks from the rattlesnakes, and tracks from the rabbits and deer. 150 yards of 7-foot-high deer fencing, and 60 post holes later, I was secure within my fortress and ready to garden.

I started with corn. In my first city-garden, I'd planted a single corn seed in a redwood tub and had been rewarded with something that looked like a 8-foot tall piece of grass. So this time I planted 200 corn seeds -- all the packet held -- not realizing that each tiny seed was a kind of Trojan horse in disguise. Precisely on July 5th, my tiny family of two had 400 mature ears of corn. The following week each of my 25 varieties of tomatoes began to produce, as did my eggplants, strawberries and zucchinis. Zucchinis, by the way, are very much like fish. As long as they live, they continue to grow, and often at alarming rates.

I haven't totalled up the cost of this hobby of mine, and my wife has had the good grace not to ask. I am sure it would be cheaper to buy everything at the store. I am shopping for a new walk-in freezer to hold our harvest, and I will be investing in another dozen cases of mason jars soon. But my proudest achievement so far is the motto I just hung over the garden gate.

Those who can, garden. And, as Mr. Mason certainly knew, those who garden, can.

The Last Ninja Bee Keeper

Our strawberry patch seems to double in size every year. What was once a manageable 10'x10' square, is now threatening to overrun the east end of our garden. This is fine with me -- there is nothing like a bowlful of freshly-picked, juicy strawberries to start off the day. The only problem is that "the yield" is way down. Healthy plants cover five times as much ground as when we started, but only produce twice as many berries. The latent cost-accountant inside me was worried. My know-it-all neighbor agreed.

"Looks like you'll have to pollinate them flowers yourself," he said with a suggestive thrust of his hips. He paused long enough for my active imagination to envision a pre-dawn raid by the SWAT team from the unnatural-acts-to-the-plants division of the Department of Agriculture.

"Or," he continued, "you could get yourself some bees."

I knew that most beekeepers move their hives around to take advantage of a variety of blossoms. My leering neighbor had some hives on his place. But I also knew his ironclad reluctance to lend anything to a fellow neighbor, especially one in need. Clearly a case of the hives and the hive-nots.

At the time I wasn't in a position to make a major investment in hives, smokers, and other equipment. Luckily, the local phone book listed a Apiarian Society and I gave them a call.

"How many do you need?" the friendly voice asked.

"I don't know."

"Fair enough. The Society is having a demonstration this afternoon. Drop on by and we'll talk about it."

How many bees would it take to pollinate a 10'x50' berry patch?

I'd seen bees in the garden before and they only spent a few seconds at any one flower. Each plant was about a foot apart, so I had 500 plants. If each plant had ten flowers, that was 5,000 flowers that needed pollinating. When I allowed for travel time between flowers, nectar breaks, lunch hours and hallway gossip, I came up with an estimated 5,000 bee-minutes worth of work.

My strawberry patch offered one bee about two weeks of steady employment, or if they preferred to work in teams (I didn't know) a two-bee team might finish in a week.

"There has got to be a Shakespeare pun in here somewhere," I droned as I dressed for the meeting, "Two bees or not two bees . . ."

I'd seen pictures of beekeepers before: pith helmet, veil, white coveralls, and gloves. I didn't have these things, and the lack reminded me of Thoreau's words, "Beware of all enterprises that require new clothes."

Anyway, I wasn't setting myself up in the bee business, I just wanted to employ a few of them part-time. I threw together my own outfit from things in the closet -- trying to make a fashion statement. White was too bland. Black was better, more mysterious. The bees would keep their distance, I thought. I donned my black sweatsuit, tightened the hood drawstrings around my chin, strapped on my safety goggles, grabbed a match box to hold my bees, and headed for the door.

"Bruce Lee film festival in town?" my wife laughed.

Five seconds after I arrived at the Apiarian Society I sensed that few successful ninjas keep bees. Agitated bees hurled themselves at my goggles until their numbers blinded me. I fell to the floor under the weight of thousands of bees as they attacked my flailing arms. It seemed like forever before I was rescued in a billowing cloud of smoke that calmed my assailants.

Bees tend to sting dark objects, I was told when I regained consciousness and the swelling had started to go down. Reminds them of bears and other honey-stealers in the wild.

Which is why pollinating time at the Clear Creek Ranch strawberry patch will be calculated in knee-minutes and not bee-minutes. I bought an artist's brush and some knee pads. I'm working my way up and down the rows hunkered over on my knees, pollinating one tingling flower at a time.

Tour de Farce

Each year from March through June the meadows surrounding the ranch are a riot of color as the trees leaf out and the wildflowers bloom: rich greens, yellows, reds, and blues. The seasonal creeks are still running and winter's muddy sediment has settled, leaving crystal clear ponds rippled by the presence of an occasional duck. Families of deer and quail graze idly, only inches from our deck. Bluebirds glide across our field of view like something from a Disney movie. Visitors arrive from the cities to the south.

All is <u>not</u> well.

Don't get me wrong. I'm always glad to see family, or old friends. And since we live a long day's drive from any other relatives, we often play host. Overnight, a weekend, sometimes longer. We developed our own packaged tour of the area . . . long circuitous routes that avoid unseemly things like front lawn auto graveyards or impromptu landfill sites.

Our routes are designed to take in the maximum of photo-opportunity scenery on the smoothest roads with a minimum of doubling back. We've even got it to where we drive by our favorite restaurants just when everyone is feeling hunger pangs. It is a well-oiled, smooth-running Chamber of Commerce-like itinerary.

But how many times can you look down the same mine shaft, or up at the same towering pine? I have seriously considered recording an audio cassette and handing our guests a map of our route, but my wife objects.

"We aren't the auto club, you know," she said.

She's right, and besides, I thoroughly enjoy showing people the area I've chosen as my home. And more than that, I enjoy all the oohs and aahs I hear, and the gushing praise that we are the luckiest people in the world, living here in "God's Country," surrounded by wildlife and fresh air.

"Did you hear how little they paid for all this?" they whisper to one another. "Mike certainly knew what he was doing when he left the city!"

Yes, I like visitors . . . as long as that is what they really are. But some people who call themselves my friends are actually house-hunters in disguise, with a secret agenda -- plans to move to a newly sub-divided paradise of their own somewhere in the neighboring forest. And they are telling all their friends where it is!

Not that those friends-of-friends will be staying with us; but the very idea of more and more city-dwellers crowding around makes me long for wide open spaces. I, for one, think we should have closed the gate to this county the day after I moved here.

Of course, the small towns I live near aren't helping the invasion situation at all. They've got these darned cute Main Streets with old brick buildings, horse-drawn carriages, quaint bed-and-breakfasts, wonderful restaurants, and (worst of all) friendly people. Let me tell you, I have my work cut out for me if I am going to stave off these swarming locust-like newcomers.

I designed a new tour applying the same attention to detail that I had to the original. It is a study in reverse psychology. I call it "Mike's Tour From Heck."

Now instead of encouraging visits during the lush months of spring, we tout the parched arid husk of late summer with its airless 100° nights. We search the byways for potholes (not hard work) and linger at the locations of hundreds of abandoned automobiles. A twilight tour of the landfill is de rigueur, as are the scorched remains of smoldering forest fires.

By arranging this new tour near the end of a visit, we are assured that our guests would return to the city with less than glowing memories of our surroundings. City living never looked so good!

Or so we thought.

They are still moving up here. They just won't talk to us anymore.

Subdivide and Conquer

The ATF might as well cancel its scheduled attack, if any, on the Clear Creek Ranch Dividians. No need to obliterate us, we are self-destructing on our own, thanks. Oh, and revise that "we" to an "I," too. My wife has arranged a sect-change operation. There goes 50% of the Dividians' person-power and an even larger share of our communal brain-trust.

For a while there we were threatening to become a modern California foothills version of one of those South Pacific cargo cults. You know . . .. Earlier this century cults popped up on isolated Pacific Islands when inhabitants became frustrated by their lack of the material goods they learned were available in the outside world. They fashioned crude full-sized wooden replicas of what was wanted: guns, airports, televisions, warehouses. The idea was to attract the real thing by combining magic and wishful thinking.

Not unlike that movie from a few years ago, Field of Dreams, where an unlikely farmer in tight jeans bulldozes a regulation baseball diamond in his corn field out in the middle of nowhere. "Build it and they will come," a magical voice whispered from somewhere offstage.

But the build-it-and-they-will-come magic doesn't always work, judging from the high vacancy rates and tenant turnover in all the new shopping centers popping up around the little town near Clear Creek Ranch. And the increased employment opportunities touted by the developers often go to managers imported from outside the area, or have a distinct minimum wage quality of life about them.

The regular generation of a living wage has long been a major concern to the inhabitants of Clear Creek Ranch. During a recent unemployed spell ("Epoch or era is more like it," my wife says) I tested out another cargo cult theory, one set forth about twenty years ago by John T. Molloy. His "Dress for Success" hypothesis is that clothes make the man. Dress as successful people in your profession dress, you will be successful too.

Once again I ignored Thoreau's warning -- beware of all enterprises that require new clothes -- and bought an expensive conservatively cut three-piece suit, dark with muted pinstripes. While waiting for the Fortune 500 firms to burn up my fax machine with lucrative offers, I spent my days idling around the ranch tying and re-tying my $200 power ascot and buffing my cordovan wingtips to a high gloss. I eventually discovered the depressing truth: guys who look like a million bucks are a dime a dozen.

But rather than genuflect along with Thoreau's mass of men leading lives of quiet desperation I decided to develop the one asset I had yet to exploit: Clear Creek Ranch itself. I would sub-divide our ten-plus acres into a hundred tiny ranch-lets.

A mini-metropolis would blossom around us among the chaparral. A quasi-religion germinated, the Clear Creek Ranch Sub-Dividians was born (again). All the tracts I would hand out were going to have buildings on them.

The development plans were magnificent to behold. They included everything a modern community seems to need: an inaccessible library with limited hours and few books, a traditional public school (and space for a dozen sore-head parent splinter group/charter school alternatives), a post office with a postage stamp-sized, yet maze-like parking lot, several mini-malls with no skateboarding allowed, nothing else for the kids to do, inadequate roads, and septic systems that only function during the dry season. I staked out the lots and built appropriate cargo cult-like structures on each. "Build it and they will come," I fervently whispered.

"They" were preceded by the money men. According to "them," the whole thing required an oppressive amount of debt financed by vaguely referenced bond issues at astronomically high interest rates payable to a web of faceless corporations. I fondled the on-off switch on my power cravat as my stockinged foot searched in vain under the conference table for a wing tip that had taken flight (along with my un-developed hopes and dreams).

Dejected, I eased into the cargo cult Maserati-like structure I had fashioned from pine cones and manzanita twigs, confident that the 120 mile an hour wind in my highly-moussed hair would soon blow those blues away. That was when my wife bailed out.

"Wacko," was all she said. How Reno-esque of her.

Of course the car wouldn't start. No gas. And I can't risk putting any in until fire season passes.

How diffi-cult.

Canning for Those Who Can't

The afternoon a whole year's worth of frozen vegetables thawed was a turning point in my life. I'd checked on the freezer after one of our regular rural power outages, and forgot to close the door. It must have been an omen or something, because since the day I left that door ajar, I have been surrounded with jars -- Mr. Mason's canning jars.

After that un-chilling experience, my wife and I warmed to the idea of canning. It might be a better way to preserve our garden harvest, along with the liberal supplement we acquired weekly from the Organic Growers' Market. Not much is happening in our garden during late summer, so it is an ideal time for canning. Our family lives by the motto, "When the growing gets tough, the tough go chopping."

Autumn activities begin with "The Ritual of the Knives." Everyone in the family has very specific roles to play. My wife begins by mentioning how dull all the knives are. I, of course, deny it. She illustrates her point by using the cutting edge of each knife to squash a ripe tomato flat without even breaking the skin. She mentions that dull knives are more dangerous than sharp knives.

"But I just sharpened them last year," I always say.

Then I take the knife and try to slice another tomato, and invariably manage to hack a few large chunks of skin off the knuckles of my holding-hand. My wife has already laid out an assortment of tourniquets and bandages, and while I hop around the kitchen yelping in pain, she selects an appropriate one and waits for my blood pressure to subside. This usually doesn't take long considering the rate at which I am losing blood.

Then, with my remaining good hand, I sharpen all the knives, while my wife assembles scientific paraphernalia such as the altitude conversion chart for boiling times, and the one that translates bushels into liters-per-footcandle. She reads aloud all the warnings about the dangers of molds, bacteria, enzymes, and botulism.

Then we leaf through the canning instruction book, looking at the "how-to" illustrations. The smiling model wears an immaculate white apron with ruffles and enough makeup for a cocktail party. She is barehanded, with a new manicure and no bandages visible. Sliced tomatoes are fanned out in perfect semi-circles on the counter, which is, of course, clean and dry. The floor isn't visible in the pictures, but I'm sure there are no cat food bowls for her to step in while juggling scalding-hot quart jars.

My wife and I look at each other, and then over at the teetering stacks of tomato flats and dusty boxes full of canning jars. We throw back our heads in unison and laugh. Eventually the giggling stops, and we swap a litany of helpful hints we have learned the hard way, like:

1. Can only what you plan to eat. Years ago we got a great deal on a few cases of persimmons. While the orange jars add a cheerful touch to our pantry shelves, I've only opened one, when I accidentally knocked it off the shelf.

2. Use the right sized jars: It defeats the purpose of preserving to use gallon jars for something you use by the eye-dropperful once a month -- unless you like growing fuzzy grey rugs on your food.

3. Meat processing rules do not necessarily apply: Like when an over-zealous cucumber grater shreds and drops gobs of his knuckle skin irretrievably into the relish mix.

(We have more, but a few of you might be getting our preserves as gifts sometime, and we'd like you to have a sense of adventure and surprise when you do.)

Finally, when we can postpone the inevitable no longer, I say, "Let's get started." And my wife, the master of timing, always remarks, "Oh gosh, I forgot the jar lids. I'll go into town for some."

It is a long way to town. She does this every year, and always returns just as I finish chopping and cooking everything. Does she do it on purpose? Should I get angry?

Canning with mason jars has taught me a valuable lesson: Once you flip your lid, it is impossible to put things back the way they were. So I keep mine screwed on tight . . . when I can, anyway.

Road Warrior

I moved from the city to the country to get some peace and quiet, and now I live a mile-and-a-half from the nearest county-maintained road. No one warned me about private road associations.

Oh, my realtor mentioned that my home was part of such an association, but she described the Disney version where once or twice a year I met with my jovial and industrious neighbors, each with a rake, a shovel, and load of gravel. We would horse around like those models in the J Crew catalog, before spending a few hours catching up on neighborhood news as we harmoniously filling a couple of potholes.

But now, several years later, long after my eyes were opened, and at least a week since the scars have healed, I offer these suggestions to anyone contemplating a safari in the asphalt jungle of road associate-dom.

◘ Privacy: remember some folks can't get enough of it. Everyone didn't move to the country for the same honorable reasons you did. Call before dropping in on an unknown neighbor, at least until you've properly classified them as desperado, misanthrope, or relatively harmless. Always stay in the truck until the dogs are chained.

◘ Meetings: will last twice as long as planned and accomplish half as much. Find a neutral, indestructible location that is far enough away from the neighborhood to discourage anyone from walking home in a fit of anger. The location should have an ample parking lot, but only one entrance/exit. Arrange to arrive last and park crosswise in the driveway to discourage anyone from ducking out early. Dress comfortably. Wear loose clothing so the bulletproof vest won't show. Earplugs and safety glasses are suggested.

Consider banning booze, smoking, sharp objects, and animals.

There is nothing worse than trying to make a serious point in front of an already hostile crowd, and having someone's lap dog hugging your ankle as he tries to mate with your argyle sock.

Small children should also be banned, although not always for the same reason.

◘ Officers: should <u>not</u> be elected "because it serves them right." Get a president who lives as far in on the road as possible. Extra points if the candidate has access to earthmoving equipment. Select a club secretary who can both hear and spell. And find a treasurer who can do sums <u>and</u> who already has a reliable source of income.

◘ Questions: never ask open-ended ones like "What does everyone think about the road?" unless you are a retired umpire aching for some action. Limit comments to ten or twenty minutes each. Does anyone really care who ran whom off the road back in '73? When all else fails remember Roberts Rules of Order. It is a nice heavy little book, but remember, too, you can only throw at someone once. It says so on page 402.

◘ Costs: Here, everyone agrees, sort of. They all agree it is going to cost too much and they disagree about how that cost should be allocated. People living at the far end of the road want the cost divided equally among the property owners; those living out near the county road want to pay by the foot; and, in their heart of hearts, nobody really wants to pay anything at all.

◘ The Real Costs: One can put a price a mile long strip of asphalt ten feet wide, providing it finally gets poured. But how does one put a price on destroyed composure, high blood pressure, and a strained marriage? And after all the tears, even if the road is beautifully paved, only one thing is guaranteed. For better or worse, your relationship with the neighbors will never be the same.

The Just-A-Minute Men

What with all the recent negative publicity in the national press, we are disbanding our neighborhood militia out here near Clear Creek Ranch. The decision was not unanimous, of course. Our group, often tightly wound-up, was never too tightly banded to start with.

How could it be? This was basically the same group that made up our road association. You remember that story: there were the pavers versus the non-pavers, and the payers versus the non-payers, and splinter groups demanding speed bumps, curbs, crossing guards, and/or street lights. The neighborhood divided itself into separate seething camps of hostility.

There were some road association meetings when calling out the militia might have restored order. But we were the militia, and we were already there -- although not armed. Checking the artillery at the door is one of the first rules for a bloodless road association meeting, and usually an effective one, we have found.

So anyway, as it happened, several of us who can read were studying cheerful books that predict natural disasters for California during the next few years: earthquakes, tsunamis, mudslides, volcanic activity, pandemic bad hair days, and some really bad stuff, too. Each of these cataclysmic events will send waves of ravenous refugees fleeing to the hills.

Our hills, not theirs. As if we weren't recent urban transplants ourselves. Although most of us didn't have to get mugged or car-jacked before we decided to move up out of the smog and fog. So we must be more intelligent, right? Not that you could discern any superfluous IQ points cluttering up one of our militia meetings.

Take the simple matter of naming our unit. The rag-tag dress of our motley group ranged from a trendy jogging outfit tie-dyed in camouflage-like earth tones, to vintage bare-armed Rambo, to lure-bristling fly-fisherman, to some sort of 21st Century electronic virtual reality-viking warlord. Given this uniform lack of uniformity, I suggested "Clear Creek Irregulars." Which was rejected as sounding too much like we were in dire need of oat bran infusions, and sparked a number of tasteless jokes about troop movements.

Everyone present had other, "better" ideas, and each was democratically debated for hours before being put to a vote. Nothing takes just a minute for these minutemen. It was a hopeless twelve-way deadlock tie, each name got one vote. So we anonymously moved onto the next order of business: maneuvers.

Most of our maneuvering consisted of parallel parking all our 4-wheel drive vehicles along one side of my neighbor's driveway for a demonstration of his heavy artillery. Then we do a little "mine" sweeping activity to locate potential patty hazards in his cow pasture which is where he keeps his homemade cannon. It lobs brightly colored bowling balls about 50 yards with reasonable accuracy, accompanied by a great deal of smoke and noise.

Other than recoiling about ten feet with each shot, the cannon is not highly mobile, being basically a tube mounted on a truck axle with two flat tires. So unless we can get the enemy to stand still in the crater that the bowling balls have formed, we may have to fall back on our armored division -- an ancient backhoe -- or our air force -- a small squadron of homing pigeon/bombers (A few of us think the birds should that be called a squab-dron).

Our first line of defense calls for chainsawing down trees to disable easy access to our private road. The neighbor living out near the county road was the logical choice to head up that project, but he only has a dinky electric chainsaw and his extension cord wouldn't quite reach the trees. We fell to bickering about whether or not to appropriate the funds to buy him a longer cord.

About all we could agree on, between cannon blasts, as we expertly maneuvered between the ice chests and the barbecue, was our opposition to gun control. We were living proof that a fully-armed, well-fed, fully-hydrated (and in some cases, over-lubricated) militia was no threat to anyone except themselves. The way things have gone out here, I'm hoping some guys on some other road a little farther down the hill, and a little closer to the "enemy" can take "them" out before "they" get up our way.

Meanwhile, our group will still be arguing about how to spell bivouac (is there a "K" in the past tense?) and whether or not GM ever built an off-road vehicle with that name.

Just A Few Finishing Touches

"You two are looking for something unique and I think I've found it," our realtor said as we turned up a bumpy dirt road. "I have to warn you, though. It's very rustic."

We were bouncing pretty good, and the road rumble made it hard for me to hear. "Did you say rusty?"

"That too," she nodded.

We pulled into a clearing in the trees and beheld our future home: Clear Creek Ranch. It was unique all right, and both rustic and rusted. Our realtor pointed to the sturdy steel roof with a burnt red finish.

"It was engineered to develop a rusty patina," she said.

"Rusty Patina, didn't he play shortstop for . . . ."

A quick wifely elbow to my ribs reminded me that not everyone shared my sense of humor. Besides, we had no humor to spare, we were going to need it all. You see, the house needed a few finishing touches. We bought the house, as is. It had no doors, plastic sheeting for windows, an incomplete bathroom, and the exterior was covered with thick, custom-milled cedar siding.

Since the house had been occupied in that condition for several years, there were dark smoke stains on the wood below the chimney, and the boards that were most exposed to the elements were either bleached grey or sunburned black. Rainstorms had washed bits of "patina" from the roof where they overflowed the gutters and splashed on the deck staining the lower portions of the walls black. One way or another, most of the cedar had lost the rosy pink and yellow charm of its fresh-cut youth.

But I knew the wood's warm natural colors lurked beneath the surface splinters and gunk, I just had no idea how to bring it out. My helpful neighbor, the one who always had spare advice, suggested sandblasting. He knew just the man, the Sandblasting Guy. Later I discovered this was my neighbor's son-in-law/debtor, and he owed my neighbor several back-payments on a loan originally taken out to purchase sandblasting equipment.

A large part of a sandblaster's equipment, I found, is made up of sand. He and his helper spent a few hours taping flattened cardboard boxes to protect our windows, and cramming articles of the clothing they were wearing into vents and flues. The helper was down to his skivvies when to my relief the Sandblasting Guy pronounced the place sufficiently corked-up.

Even so, we later discovered tiny sand-drifts around the house from pinhole-sized cracks in the construction. They donned what looked like deep sea diving suits and aimed a fire hose arrangement at the house. In less than two hours, the siding looked great. But I had no time to enjoy my new title: Mike, the Patina Turner.

"The secret is to keep it looking great," my neighbor said, and I braced myself for another relative sales pitch.

If I left the wood unprotected, he told me, I'd have to sandblast every few years and I couldn't do that indefinitely. He pointed out that the siding was a lot thinner now, and figured we'd loose 15 points of R-value with every blast.

I soon found myself at the Clear Wood Preserver Guy's store. Since I wanted to see the natural color of the wood, I got a dozen barrels of something that looked and smelled a lot like gasoline. I mixed it with equal parts of linseed oil and proceeded to spread it liberally over the walls and, inadvertently, myself.

It must work, I haven't chipped, cracked, or faded yet. One drawback was that I couldn't man the barbecue for several weeks each year until my coating either dried or wore off.

But the BIG problem was "each year" -- the stuff had to be applied annually, which I did religiously for two whole years. The third year I just did the walls that show when visitors drive up. The fifth year it was only the walls that took the worst beating from the elements. And now . . . now I am paying the price. Yes, we are suffering patina-creep again. And my neighbor is talking about somebody he might know called the Aluminum Siding Guy.

Up The Creek Without a Puddle

According to our real estate agent the little creek here at Clear Creek Ranch gets its name from the fact that you can always see the creek bottom clearly. Which is true, as far as it goes. I soon discovered that for nine months of the year, I can reach down at random and touch the creek bed without any risk of getting wet at all. It seems our agent left out a key word when describing the creek: seasonal.

The problem with seasonal creeks (or nature's storm drains) is that they only exist during the rainy season, which happens to be an uncomfortable season to enjoy water sports out here. I have yet to jump in the water to cool off in the dead of winter when I am already soaked to the skin and shivering.

We built a dam pond with the help of the Pond Guy in hopes of trapping some of the runoff, but over the years several acres of dust and dirt have decided to finish their sedimental journey right there, creating a sort of shallow, swampy mud flat -- perfect for mosquitoes and not much else.

A spring on the far edge of our property dribbles along at the rate of a gallon a minute. Hardly a babbling brook, according to the Spring Development Guy, but he claimed the water could be piped uphill and upstream for us. Given the length of our creek and the slow natural flow rate of the spring, he figured that during the summer heat he could deliver enough liquid to keep the sand in the creek bed moist -- in the shade anyway.

The clincher was the price tag, roughly equal to the factory sticker on a new luxury automobile that the Spring Development Guy probably had his eye on.

The old right-of-way that leads down to our mailboxes on the county road crosses and re-crosses an impressively full irrigation canal. I phoned the local irrigation district to see about hooking up. An official-sounding voice answered.

"How many inches do you need?" she asked.

"Inches? Just a minute, let me think," I said.

What an odd way to calculate it, I thought. But it was no weirder than some of the county building department's requirements. At least it wasn't metric. It's about a mile to my place, that's 5,280 feet, and (where was my calculator?) about 63,360 inches. I rounded it off to be safe.

"65,000 inches," I said confidently.

I heard a strangling noise on the other end, then the sound of something crashing to the floor, uncontrollable giggling, and something about "up periscope."

Soon another voice, male this time, came on the phone and helped me fathom the arcane terminology associated with rural water delivery. The "inches" were miner's inches (worth 11.2 gallons per minutes each), a holdover from the days when the area's gold seekers used hydraulic mining techniques. What I had ordered was enough water to keep all of the ranch, including the hilltops, submerged for a long, long, time.

I down-sized my inches, assumed an alias, affected a limp, and made an appointment to review my case with the irrigation district. Unfortunately, their ditch maps outline topography and not parcels or building lots. After hours of study I spotted a landmark we could use (a pre-historic auto graveyard dumping canyon) and by triangulation we located Clear Creek Ranch. Irrigation canals snaked their way through canyons all around me. Surely this was going to be easy!

The Irrigation District Guy sighed that sigh. The delivery problem was grave, or at least had to do with gravity. Even though several irrigation ditches were nearby, they were downhill from my property and I'd have to pay to install a mile of pipe

24

and some pumping stations to get any water -- provided the many landowners between the ditch and my place agreed to let me lay the pipe. Several of these neighbors were also on the other side (losing side) in recent heated discussions at our road association. I knew that the only way they would let me bury irrigation pipe on their land was if they could bury me along with it.

Which is why, for the time being anyway, if you stroll along our creek in the late summertime, the only babbling you'll hear will be coming from me.

Kick Back

As a lifelong city boy, my first exposure to chainsaws came at the movies. You know the ones -- where good-looking teenagers in bad need of acting lessons receive involuntary amputations from some masked psychopath with a southern accent.

Many years later, when we purchased Clear Creek Ranch, the former owner left us his old greasy chainsaw. The thing weighed about 200 pounds. It seemed more like a car engine with a hand-grip. The bar was about four feet long and covered with a menacing row of freshly-sharpened saw teeth. No tree on my property stood a chance. Providing I could lift it, which I couldn't.

"This here's a housewarming gift," his friendly note said. "Better cut some firewood soon if you want the house to stay warm."

My wife pointed to our empty woodbox and to the snowflakes that were sticking to our cats as they waited outside the door. The temperature was dropping.

Since I couldn't carry the saw to the logs, I rolled the logs to the saw and then spent an hour getting the engine started. In retrospect, "logs" may be too strong a term. How about branches? Or maybe twigs on steroids?

I set the "logs" on the ground in front of the saw and tipped it forward. Sparks and wood chips flew. When nothing flew anymore I stopped the engine. The once menacing sawteeth were gone. The chain was smooth enough to go on a bicycle.

Later, the Chainsaw Repair Guy would point out (in a rather caustic way) what an inefficient trenching tool a chainsaw is. But at that moment, I was delighted with the small mound of "firewood" by my side. I'd probably call it kindling today. But the length was uniform: I used a tape measure and a pencil to mark each piece before I cut it.

We spent hours getting the wood into the house, not because there was so much, but because we had to find the camera and then the film, and then stage a shot of each of us carrying the first loads of firewood into our new home. By morning all my precisely cut fuel had been burned.

I spent most of the next day learning how to install the spare saw chain without a manual. Then I rounded up all the remaining firewood possibilities and by nightfall had another stack of wood and another bicycle chain. We didn't take as many pictures that day.

On the third day my wife suggested that a portable chainsaw might work well. What a novel idea!

The Chainsaw Sales Guy said I could solve my bicycle chain symptoms with a sawbuck, which I found out a little later is not a ten dollar bill, but an X-shaped rig for keeping the wood off the ground so the logs can fall on your shins as you saw them off. Then his eyes lit up as he talked about kickback, which I was relieved to find out was not a bribe.

"Kickback is no football play, or dance step," he said. "And it sure doesn't mean relax. Just the opposite! The saw tip can bounce back from one of those widow-maker knots and take your head off like that!" he laughed ghoulishly. "Blood spurting everywhere!"

Did I detect a psychopathic southern accent?

The Chainsaw Sales Guy had no "head guards" or "widow-maker detectors" in stock, but he did have an orange hardhat in my size, complete with earmuffs and a plexiglass face shield. He also talked me into this apron-chaps thing made of bulletproof material that might save me from sawing my own leg off by accident. We selected a medium-sized chain saw.

And as a small crowd of amused store clerks looked on, he coached me in the "proper" foot placement and rigid straight-arm technique to avoid the dreaded kickback. It seemed like an unnatural position at the time. Later, after four hours of chainsawing, every muscle in my body told me it was.

It wasn't until I was shopping in the Yellow Pages for a chiropractor to undo the damage that I realized every one of them had the same last name as the Chainsaw Sales Guy.

Talk about the danger of kickbacks!

There's Always A Hitch

Scrap 2x4s were our main fuel the first year we had a woodstove. Even then I knew it wasn't proper fuel, but the square wood was easy to stack and it kept us warm.

When all the construction scraps were gone I bought a chainsaw to take advantage of the "free" firewood growing on our property. Well actually, I bought a chainsaw, an extra chain, a scabbard to protect the chain on the saw, an electric saw sharpener, heavy gloves, orange hardhat, safety goggles, ear plugs, fuel and a fuel can, two kinds of oil, and this heavy apron/chaps thing to protect my legs. All I needed was a squire to help me up onto my sawhorse and I was ready to joust with the trees in my quest for the lost cord.

As a novice, I only picked on fallen trees. I figured it was pretty hard to get squashed by something that is already laying on the ground. Soon I was surrounded by stack after stack of neatly sawn 18-inch logs.

At the end of the day, when my saw and I were both out of gas, one of my neighbors came over to see what all the noise was about. When he saw my woodpile, he smirked.

"That's no way to stack wood," he laughed, and gave the nearest pile a nudge with his boot. It was a domino effect. Logs toppled, hitting the second pile, which toppled into the third. Soon logs were rolling everywhere. I suddenly realized that I own very little level land.

"You need criss-cross cribbing on the ends for stability," he said. "Take a look at one of my piles next time you drive by."

As I rounded up my stray logs I thought about kicking his pile over, but quickly reconsidered. After all, he had been on the rational side (my side) during the road association negotiations. And who knew where a rural log-kicking feud might lead. So I inspected his arrow-straight rows of precisely stacked oak. I nudged the pile, it felt like it was nailed together.

Criss-cross cribbing is hard to stack without splitting the logs, they keep rolling away. So I bought a maul, which is like an axe, but it has a heavy wedge-shaped head that makes log splitting easier, although not necessarily easy.

A vicious circle swirled in my brain: I wanted dry firewood. I had green, wet logs. Split wood dries faster than whole logs.

But green wood is harder to split than dry wood, which if I had, I wouldn't need to split. A splitting headache began to throb behind my eyes.

My wrists and lower back gave out about the time the blisters on my palms broke, which was right after I split my last cribbing log. Three days later, after several hundred dollars of massage-therapy, I regained partial use of my back and hands. With a stiff finger, I dialed up my neighborhood expert to keep him current on the firewood situation.

"Get yourself a hydraulic splitter, son," he drawled. "I'd lend you mine, but you know how it is with lending tools to neighbors."

I had ten times more wood left to split and no energetic teenaged son to send out there to do it. So I went shopping for a log splitter.

I found that for the cost of a dozen cords of seasoned oak, delivered, split, and stacked at my door step, I could purchase a light-weight log splitter. The Splitter Sales Guy assured me it would last a lifetime, which gave me or the splitter at least a ten year life span just to break even since we only burn about a cord a year.

He wanted me to consider a small tractor to haul the splitter to job sites on my property, and a trailer to haul the finished product back to the house. I would need to pay extra for warranties, insurance on everything, and maintenance agreements since I'm not mechanically inclined. Oh, and I'd need a new $50 trailer hitch assembly for my truck to haul all my new toys home, where I knew I'd have to spend several weekends building a new storage shed to house all this labor-saving stuff.

I made a mental note to leave room in the new shed for the rototiller I needed for my garden. Suddenly firewood preparation was going to cost me more than my kids' entire college education. Dazed and babbling, I begged the salesman for moment alone with my checkbook.

Well, following much soul-searching and gnashing of teeth, I finally did it. I wrote him a check . . . for a whopping $50.

Then I swung by the local rental yard, and towed home a rented log splitter on my brand new trailer hitch.

The Noisy Art of Forgery

We have no spreading chestnut trees here at Clear Creek Ranch, which may explain why there was no village smithy standing around when I needed one -- not to lend a "large and sinewy hand," but to give advice on the set of fireplace tools (poker, shovel, and tongs) I planned to build from scratch from a few iron rods. What could be more simple?

The advice my non-existent blacksmith might have given would be, "Go buy a completed set at the hardware store," but I, like Longfellow's hero, wanted to "owe not any man." And besides, I already had too many irons in the fire and new tools scattered about to pay attention to anything as simple as that. I had anvils to lift, fires to stoke, eyebrows to singe.

Part of the fun of being self-sufficient (or at least creating the illusion of self-sufficiency) is doing things "the old way." This usually means re-discovering tools and techniques from by-gone eras and applying them to current problems around the house. It also means learning a bunch of arcane terminology and acquiring a set of skills that may not get much use and developing a set of muscles that haven't been used heretofore in years, if ever.

Yes, the simple life can be complicated.

I located a hundred-pound anvil at an estate sale and lugged over to its permanent placement (I'm sure not moving it again!) on a tree stump near the shed in a shaded area. There may have been better locations, but none that offered such ideal acoustic possibilities: every hammer blow would send a resounding high-pitched clang echoing down the canyon directly toward my neighbor's house. There is nothing so satisfying (and ultimately futile) as annoying an annoying neighbor.

The estate sale also yielded a large box filled with a bewildering assortment of hammers, tongs, chisels, punches, hardies, fullers, flatters, swages, beaks, and things with really odd names. I dropped the box on the ground next to the anvil and listened as the resulting clatter echoed loudly.

The next step was to rig a forge to fire things up. I chose the family barbecue. It hadn't had much use since we became vegetarians. Bits of petrified tofu from our last al fresco fiasco still clung to its now-rusty grill.

In a nod toward modern convenience, I installed an old electric hairdryer-blower in place of the tradition hand-cranked bellows. Soon the coals were glowing red-hot. In a nod toward the wisdom of the ages, the plastic housing on the hairdryer demonstrated how quickly it could melt.

For the better part of the next three days I heated, pounded, twisted, punched, riveted, howled, smoldered, and cajoled those once-perfectly straight pieces of metal into a variety of shapes that might have been more at home in a cubist painting, or possibly standing alongside the gargoyles on, say, Steven King's roof.

No matter that my hands were scorched and cracked and bleeding, that my forearm muscles were bulging and foreshortened, and that my fingers, tensed from gripping the hammer were unable to hold a coffee cup. My work was done!

The hinged tongs moved easily, although due to the weight, it took two of us to operate them. The fact that the ends didn't meet, or even pass near to each other, added to their rustic charm (a term I find works well with so many of my projects). I've offered to make sets for friends, but they always decline the offer. "Tongs, but no tongs," they say.

And the poker, with its pointed end and curved barb was on a scale that Captain Ahab would have been quite comfortable with, as he rammed it home into Moby Dick's blubber. How this harpoon worked with our petite Jötul woodstove is another matter.

I gave up on the shovel altogether, although I did complete the handle. Early in the day when I'm strongest, I can still lift it all by myself and it actually makes a better fire poker than the one I crafted for that purpose.

And I wonder if perhaps that's not what Longfellow was referring to when he ended that blacksmith poem "Something attempted, something [else] done, has earned a night's repose?"

I think it was, but let me sleep on it.

Bean and Nothingness

Summer is barbecue season here at Clear Creek Ranch. We use manzanita twigs gathered from our ten acres instead of buying charcoal. I figure the place will no longer be a fire hazard when we use up all the twigs in about 150 years. Luckily, my wife likes the taste that the manzanita smoke imparts to the food, and to the cook. If anyone out there has test results showing that manzanita smoke is carcinogenic, please don't write to me.

Our Independence Day barbecue was heck the year we went vegetarian -- the tofu kept falling through those cracks in the grill. We have since discovered the tofu hot dog which feels and tastes just like the "real thing" when slathered with mustard -- and it isn't chock-full of chemicals, dyes, snouts, ears, hooves and miscellaneous body parts.

If I had an extra wish, I'd wish that tofu had a better name. It sounds so foreign and exotic. Calling it soybean curd doesn't work either. Curd just isn't a proper word for a food. I will try to use it in some sentences.

"Excuse me, but you stepped in a pile of curds out in the yard, and you are tracking it all over my new rug."

"Oh, dear, I know how unsightly that can be! Why once I accidentally squished around in a curd barefooted and I was picking the foo out of my toes for weeks."

Tofu has a severe image problem (undeserved) and it doesn't stop with the name. Unfortunately, there is no historical romance connected with bean curds in our culture. The only popular story involving beans at all, incorrectly makes them the symbol of stupidity during the early going.

I am speaking of "Jack and the Beanstalk." Jack was awarded a dunce cap in the first part of that story when he traded all that animal protein (a cow) for a puny handful of beans. Nutritionally speaking, Jack had the right idea, he just didn't make a fair trade.

He'd have been okay if he got several sacks of beans, and a wheel barrow, because his vegetable protein certainly wasn't going to walk home by itself like its animal cousin could. The whole thing, of course, is part of a longstanding scheme of the bovine cholesterol/protein propaganda machine.

The Old West still captures the American public's imagination, largely due to too many hours frittered in front of the TV.

We all have memories of a mythical time dominated by thirty-minute morality plays involving cattle culture and cowboys. To my knowledge there is no vegetable equivalent -- no lean, sunburned beanboys wearing beanskin chaps who tamed the west by wielding matched pairs of pearl-handled pea shooters.

If beans were the dominant protein in the old West, billionaire bean barons would have imported Swiss watchmakers to manufacture the tiny branding irons needed to keep indeterminate bean vines from wandering into the neighbor's yard. Would there have been bean drives to Boston? There certainly would be no picturesque bean bones bleaching in the sun. (Modern-day beans have had the bones bred out of them.)

Rodeos -- those fairground favorites -- would not exist as we know them today. They would be much more civilized, leisurely indoor events, involving bean-picking rather than bulldogging contests, burrito wrapping instead of calf roping, and pinto beans rather than pinto ponies.

National Geographic would run pictorials and PBS would feature a series about the eminent demise of wild bean varieties known as mustangs. Perhaps if the fortunes of beef and beans were reversed, we would use expressions like "useless as a hill of beef." For politeness' sake I have omitted all references to the expletive "bull!" and its many variations, which would enjoy a much smaller place in all our vocabularies if the bean were king.

I may be fighting a losing fight here. My revisionist protein history is probably too radical for many of you. But it may give you "food for thought" the next time dad is out there torching a bonfire in the patio, scorching the hair off his arms, and living up to the barbecuer's motto: "If it's smokin', it's cookin'; when it's black, it's done."

Feed A Fever

A recent trip to the dentist saw me enduring a root canal and acquiring a gold crown. This took quite a bite out of my savings, which in turn gave me the inspiration to root around one of the canals here at Clear Creek Ranch in hopes of striking it rich (or at least breaking even on my dental bill). You see I live in the center of what is known as "the gold country," where everyone likes to think they live on a potential bonanza. In reality most of the bonanzas split about 100 years ago, leaving a rocky road for those who followed.

But this didn't matter to me. It didn't even matter that I could never remember whether the word placer in "placer mining" rhymed with racer or with passer. Since image is everything, I immediately set about getting together the proper look.

To me all prospectors looked like cowboy movie actor Gabby Hayes. I practiced being grouchy and saying things like "consarn it" and "dangity-dang." Prospectors had beards. I quit shaving. Prospectors had picks and shovels. I raided the garden shed. Prospectors had gold pans. I finished off the last of the pie and rinsed off my precision mining instrument. Prospectors had pack animals. I rented my neighbor's burro.

"What's the difference between a burro and a donkey?" my wife asked.

I was ready for her with dictionary definitions. "A burro is a small donkey," I said, "while a donkey is a domestic ass."

"No comment," she smirked.

"I prefer the term burro," I continued, "because of it's onomatopoeic association with the minerly verb 'to burrow'."

"I can dig it," she said anachronistically.

But I was the one who did all the digging on my backyard mining expedition. My wife's sole contributions were to go to town for a loaf of sourdough bread, and to name the burro Donkey Ho-tee.

"Watch out for windmills," she said as I tried to kick-start my pack animal for a trip down to the gulch. Reverse and park were working well, but I could never get him out of low gear when it came to going forward.

"Try a carrot on a stick," my wife suggested.

That made sense to me, since it was carats that was motivating me at the moment.

Meanwhile down in the gulch (actually it was later, but all those old western movies always have a subtitle that says "meanwhile"), I found a tight bend in the creek where a lot of sand and gravel had built up. My miner's bible, "Old Zebediah's How to Pan Gold for Fun & Profit" insisted this was a likely spot. And it was, for a 100-years-worth of rusty sardine cans, bits of barbed wire, and broken glass, as well as several tons of sand.

My instructions were to gently swish and swirl the sand in my pan under running water. Clear Creek, which passes through the gulch can hardly be said to be "running" even at the height of our short rainy season. Strolling or crawling is more like it. It was in its "dry creek" phase at the time of my expedition. I loaded Donkey Ho-tee with several sackfuls of pay-dirt and spent the afternoon going uphill toward a water faucet.

The next day at dawn, refreshed and still determined, I spent hours developing carpal-tunnel-syndrome in both wrists as I repeatedly swirled my pie pan under the running tap. At dusk, my hands hanging useless at my sides, I gazed at the small pile that remained. There were no gold flakes as the book had promised, only black sand. Black sand, it said, was iron pyrite, the same thing I'd collected as a child by twirling a magnet in the dirt.

I was depressed and despondent. I said a final "con-sarn the dangity-dang blame thing." I grabbed a straight razor, admiring its sharp edge, ready to end it all. Soon I had shaved off every trace of my scruffy prospector's beard.

As for gold, it may be in them thar hills, but so far all that glisters (that was Cervantes' quixotic word choice) here at Clear Creek Ranch is on my lower left molar, second from the end.

If You Need Anything, Don't Whistle

Excepting characters in a Broadway musical, very few people burst into song at the onset of a personal emotional weather front. While I would like to credit good upbringing for this admirable display of restraint in revealing every nuance of one's rich inner life to an inquiring public, I suspect the real reasons are a lack of proximity to an adequate orchestra, illegible cue cards, or the absence of a six-figure book deal.

The more reserved among us may display subtle facial evidence of our mood swings: we smile, or frown, or grimace as the occasion merits. More demonstrative types may actually hug and kiss (or punch senseless) anything or anyone close enough to grab. The musically-inclined may hum an appropriate ditty. But humming is difficult to do at high volume and the vibrations rarely extend far beyond the hummer, thus hum-bugging no one.

Not so with whistlers -- those tune-throttling, tranquility-shattering, aural-oversteppers. In the right setting, a "good" whistler, whose little pucker only a mother could love, can annoy more folks than a boombox in a funeral parlor. Those "bassers" who drive around town in stereo speakers on wheels with the volume cranked up high (or is it low?) enough to liquify their remaining brain cells are considerate neighbors by comparison.

I don't know if 19th century American painter James Abbott McNeill Whistler was a whistler, but if he was that would explain why that famous painting of his parents only includes his mother. Dad no doubt went bonkers at his son's incessant tootling and wandered out of the room early on. Moms were, and often are, more indulgent with their children, so she alone sat still for the portrait.

If you look closely you will notice her rather stoic demeanor. Is she struggling to remain "on her rocker," or is she wishing for some sort of primitive earplugs she can screw in to deaden the pain? Perhaps she is hoping for an out-of-body experience, or at least an out-of-room one like her husband is enjoying. Certain art historians take this as further evidence that Whistler was indeed a whistler.

In case you haven't gotten it yet, I feel that public whistling should be a capital crime -- a hanging (by the lips) offense. Perpetrators should be dealt with swiftly and severely. They are as criminal as those who wantonly break wind in crowded elevators. Windbreakers who then compound their heinous offense by bursting into whistle in such close quarters have signed their own death warrant. If they aren't torn into tiny pieces before the elevator reaches its destination there is no justice.

I have observed numerous whistlers in my time, many of them in department stores. Shoppers while shopping are more prone to this solitary vice than are, say, long distance runners, who seem to favor the wheeze. Based on personal experience most whistlers are men. But in this age of equal opportunity there is nothing to stop pursed-lipped females from becoming equally annoying.

Some common whistling types to watch for:

The Monotone -- only knows one note, or can only hit one note. Emits a variety of short and long blasts not unlike Morse code in an attempt at song.

The Locked-Out in Florida -- keyless and off-key. Usually attempting (poorly) some obscure mystery melody that would challenge even Pavarotti.

The Channel Hopper -- not a bad whistler, can carry a tune, but shifts songs with each successive breath. Related to:

The Puckerus-Interruptus -- a truly great whistler with great taste in songs who gets distracted in the middle of a well-known riff and never completes it. Leaves everybody within earshot dangling, waiting for the other note to drop.

The Pestilent Melody from Heck -- a journeyman whistler who favors catchy tunes from yesteryear. The song was great the first 5,000 times you heard it twenty years ago, but now it's stuck in your brain and you can't get rid of it no matter what you do. Such as the refrain from that novelty tune: "When those cotton bolls get rotten you can't pick very much cotton, in them ol' cotton fields back home . . ."

I need to stuff some of them bolls in my ears real soon.

Going With The Flow

When we moved to the country to get "back to basics," I had no idea how basic it was going to be. And at the same time the terminology is so obscure, especially for someone like me, who will drive fifty miles the wrong way rather than ask for directions. I hate to ask questions I don't already know the answers to.

Take the term perk'n'mantle, as in "Yep, we passed the perk'n'mantle test." For all I knew, it referred to some quaint country custom, origin unknown, that requires the coffee pot to be stored neatly on that ledge above the fireplace when the building inspector finally shows up.

We had avoided most of the building inspector ordeal by buying a partially complete house.

"Got a brand new, 1,500 gallon septic tank out there," the realtor had smiled. "Just right for a small family like yours."

I assumed she was referring to the number of people in our family. Although she might have been poking fun at me, referring to my stature, which, for those of you who don't know me, isn't too tall. But, of course, I'll never really know what she meant -- as I say before, I hate to ask clarifying questions.

I did some quick mental math: at 5 gallons a flush that made 300 flushes, which would take a lot less than a year to use up at

1,500 gallons of capacity, no matter how conservative we were. Even if I retro-fitted the master bath with one of those space-age johns that uses an ecologically sound two eyedropper's-ful per flush and we always availed ourselves of the gas station facilities when we were in town, we were going to be overflowing in no time.

"And after it fills?" I asked, hoping the terror wasn't creeping into my voice.

"Oh, it drains out to the leaches."

Leeches! Little bloodsucking, worm-like parasites! Out there in our yard! Black-and-white visions influenced by years of pre-colorized old movies danced in my fevered brain: Katherine Hepburn swoons as a weary bewhiskered Humphery Bogart uses a smoldering cigarette butt to burn a writhing leech off a pale, hairy leg (not Katherine's as I recall). Or was that William Holden Kwai-ing himself a river on another sound stage, in the same war and same side, different continent and enemy?

"You know," my realtor said, "leach-lines. They're out there under the lawn."

I nodded to her as wisely as I could. She pointed out the location on a plot map that came with the blueprints. There was the square septic tank, and spreading out from it, something that looked like a badly bent television antennae.

"Have it pumped out every four or five years," she said.

I promptly forgot everything she said until five years and one day later. One of my friendly neighborhood experts had just finished supervising me as I single-handedly stacked the last of five cords of wood in firm, tightly packed rows a few yards from the house. I had secretly looked up the term "cord" in the dictionary when no one was looking, so I knew I had just stacked a total of 640 cubic feet of dry oak on my lawn.

"I'd like to help you, son," he had drawled. "But your sense of accomplishment will be much greater if you do it on your own."

I was sweating profusely and thanking him for the loan of his managerial skills when my wife interrupted to tell us we were have "that problem" again. The plumbing had been backing up regularly for over a month. My neighbor sensed another

supervisorial opportunity and began probing. He soon pronounced his diagnosis.

"Time to dig that sucker up and pump it dry," he said, adding with a pitying look, "Too bad about all that work we did today."

I let his "we" remark slide because suddenly I had an intuitive flash. I didn't need to ask anyone a question. I knew -- he had once told me he helped the contractor dig the footings and the septic system for my house, and I knew the septic tank must lay somewhere at the other end of his gaze . . . buried directly beneath my neat new wood pile.

Why Roofing Makes Me Tired

We have reopened the "form versus function" debate out here at Clear Creek Ranch. The last big storm that blew through took a few more of the garden gazebo's shingles with it. I prefer to call the new opening a rustic skylight, but my wife considers it more of a gaping hole. And, according to her, covering it up with a piece of bright blue tarp held on with duct tape just won't do. Not even for "a little while." She knows how long that can be around here.

The whole thing seems like kind of a waste. I mean we never sit out in the gazebo when any serious weather is going on. We aren't going to get wet or frozen, or even sunburned out there, because we're almost never there. It was too much trouble even when the roof was good.

We tried. At the end of a hard day we'd get all settled in, and start gazing out of our gazebo. When we were almost relaxed, one of us would need a cool drink, or something to read, or the non-cellular telephone would ring back in the house, or the mosquitos would choose us as the main course.

We decided against wood shake shingles for a couple of reasons. The "natural" untreated ones are a bit of a fire hazard. And I knew if I did try to split our own shakes from some of the likely logs in the ranch woodpile I'd have to use my froe.

Now a froe is L-shaped and is like a straight razor fixed to a short handle with the sharp edge of the razor facing down. You place that edge on the end of the log, and whack the dull edge with a wooden mallet. Then, in theory anyway, shingles (and little or no blood) are supposed to appear.

Contrary to popular belief, froe-whacking is not everyday behavior out here at Clear Creek Ranch. So that nosy neighbor of mine with nothing else to do will come over and ask me what I'm doing. I will say, "Whacking my froe." He will ask, "What froe?" I will answer, "This froe."

To and fro we will go until he thinks for a moment and then insists that "Froe!" is what dyslexic golfers yelp when they whack their balls. "You mean dyslexic floggers, don't you?" I will ask, explaining that golf and flog are anagrams too.

At which point he will wonder if anagrams aren't some sort of important bulletins from my wife, Anna (whose name, by the way, is spelled the same forward or backward). And I will announce, "Pun my word, I have a 'splitting' headache and am about to froe up."

Which is why there will be no shake roof for our gazebo. We (my wife and I, without any meaningful help from our neighbor) finally settled on some recycled roofing materials we already had around the Ranch. Resilient, insect-resistant, waterproof -- in short, old tires.

Oh, now give me some credit! I know more than a few of you are already picturing me tossing some bald old whitewalls up on the gazebo and calling it a day. For your information, I was the only bald thing up on that roof, and it took a heck of a lot longer than a day to complete this job. Nothing ever comes easy out here at Clear Creek Ranch.

As that great philosopher of my youth, Ricky Nelson warned, and I quote, "Fools rush in, where angels fear to tread." Cutting tire treads up into one foot shingle sections on a band saw borders on the foolish. And one certainly needs an angel, preferably of the guardian type, when that whirling band saw blade pops loose.

Covering our 12'x16' roof with foot-long tire sections required 640 "tiles." Or in layman's terms, 90 non-steel-belted tires worth. Which put a small dent in the supply we had from a pre-existing dump at the edge of our property.

Using the same technique as is utilized to install those curved terra cotta roofing tiles (alternating rows of upwardly- and downwardly-facing tiles), and with an unsolicited supervisorial assist from my nosy neighbor, I eventually got the job done.

Of course my wife complimented me on the installation, while at the same time observing (to no one in particular, although I was the only one there) that she had never before noticed that all tires weren't the same shade of black.

So now I'm scheduled to coat the gazebo roof with tire black several times a season. Which isn't so bad actually, except it takes several gallons of the stuff. And since tires are associated with mileage, there has got to be a miles-to-the-gallon joke in here somewhere.

But you know what? Suddenly I'm too tired to think about it.

Bridge Over Rubbled Waters

There is nothing like a rainy spring day at home. When the water descends in billowing sheets so thick and furious that one is delighted to have an empty dance card. Glad to be indoors, dry and idle, with a good book and a warm fire nearby. A quiet afternoon with no sound other than raindrops upon rooftop.

On a recent afternoon that could be described a lot like the one above, only colder, I finished checking our storm supplies in case of power failure: lanterns, candles, rain-filled five gallon buckets to act as an emergency "flushing system," and a large container of drinking water.

Drinking water -- I was thirsty. I turned on the tap for a drink of icy well water, not wishing to deplete our emergency stores. All I got was a dry sulfurous belch from my rebellious plumbing, and (no pun intended) a sinking feeling. What was going on? We had power, but no water -- a rare occurrence for us, usually everything goes out at once.

After consulting a dog-eared Bartlett's amid the tumbling stacks that comprise the ranch library, and making sure it was Coleridge who almost said "Wattage, wattage everywhere nor any drop to drink," I girded my ample loins. Nor did I stop there. I girded everything girdible in hopes that a delay would allow the storm to abate.

Yellow raingear swathed me from top to bottom and stem to stern, clammy knee-high wellington boots encased my lower reaches, and a battered campaign hat was strapped firmly under my chins. My hands, clad in hot pink dishwashing gloves, glowed as if with premature chapped-ness.

I was the Ancient Mariner, and in place of his accursed albatross, my wife fixed a plastic bag around my neck. It contained all the tools I might need to repair the pipeline damage that must be out there somewhere. I'd need my hands free for the slippery climb down to the pond adjacent to our well.

It was noon when I said, "This will only take a minute."
I descended the steep path, sometimes on foot, often on rump, finally rolling to a stop at the foot bridge spanning the spillway of our little pond. What is usually a mossy trickle had become

a roaring torrent of muddy, debris-laden water, several feet deep. So deep it covered our fresh water pipe, which for reasons only Rube Goldberg could explain, has always been suspended beneath the bridge, where it regularly freezes solid during cold snaps.

This time it had simply snapped. The force of the water had swept manhole-sized stepping stones from the pond and hurled them against the PVC pipe and over the spillway, and was continuing to do so. Rather than face the immediate uphill battle of returning home, I sat on the bridge waiting for the waters to ebb.

Soon I began to discover the many chinks in my armor against the elements. There was a wellspring in my wellingtons, my wool stockings acted like wicks, quickly drawing moisture upward from tiny holes near my boot heels until I was sodden from the knees down. Repeated skids down the hill had torn gaping holes in the rear of my rainpants. I was soon soaking wet from the waist down, but (lucky me) my hands were nice and dry.

Incorrectly assuming that the PVC solvent used to fuse plastic pipe together would work equally well on my raingear, I slathered some on and pressed the torn flaps together. I discovered how well it stuck things, not only to each other, but to my jeans and raincoat as well. The fingers of my rubber gloves fused into mutant mitten-like claws. I became the King Midas of stickiness -- everything I touched became a permanent part of my wardrobe.

Eventually the waters receded enough for me to repair the break. But I couldn't move freely in my re-sealed outfit and had to shuck it all. Some of it was stuck to the bridge anyway. Armed with hacksaw, a length of pipe, and what was left of the solvent. I crawled in the muck beneath the bridge in my underwear and rain hat. It really was a two minute repair job once I got close enough to perform it.

I returned home after dark to sounds of flowing water -- but this time it was hot, being drawn into the bathtub by my wife for me. She didn't mention the hours that had elapsed, or ask about my missing pants, or point out the shreds of plastic I'd somehow glued to my hair.

She'd seen me return from the Mr Fix-it Wars too many times for anything to surprise her.

The Finer Points of Morris Code

Last year I finally made good on a New Year's Resolution from 1987. I spent the day cleaning off my workbench in the garage here at Clear Creek Ranch. Gone were the mounds of sawdust and lumber scraps that were home to generations of field mice. Recovered were the long-lost chisels, screwdrivers, and more bent nails than I care to admit I probably produced.

As I paused to admire the rows of hand tools momentarily hung in the proper place on the wall, my wife peeked in. And while she celebrated my fleeting victory over the forces of entropy and inertia, there was a price. Her hand held a mail order brochure, and she had a woodworking request.

"Our wedding anniversary is coming up," she said, "and I wonder if you could build a Morris chair for me. Handmade gifts mean so much more, don't they?"

Stunned, I nodded in agreement. If she wanted me to build anything for the house after "The Fiasco of the Wiggling Bookcases," well, who was I to refuse? Though I had no idea what a Morris chair was.

Since my wife spends her every waking moment (and many of mine) working with the Pet Adoption League, I assumed the Morris she referred to was that grumpy orange tomcat that shills for a pet food company. What kind of "chair" could a cat need? I pictured old Morris curled up in a simple box with a pillow in it. Even I could build a box, given two or three tries.

My wife soon informed me that a Morris chair is no such thing. It was named after William Morris who was an English designer, and poet among other things, and a founder of the Arts and Crafts movement. His namesake chair is of the "easy" variety, with an adjustable back and removable cushions.

Hmmm, this was going to be a challenge. I had never built anything whose parts moved intentionally, and certainly not in a predetermined direction. I toyed with the possibility of just buying her the chair.

The one pictured in the catalog was comfortable looking, squarish, with simple lines, "Mission style." This boxy chair was fashioned from either teak wood or Honduran mahogany, covered with leather, and ours for only $1,400 plus a "modest" shipping fee. "Mission impossible is more like it," my anemic checkbook gasped.

"Leather?" I queried with raised eyebrow -- I sensed a loophole through which to escape immediate pauperhood. We like to keep animals and their skins together around here.

"Of course not," she replied. "The cloth-covered one is less expensive. A rainforest floral print, only $1,250."

"Politically-correct and thrifty too!" I thought as I weighed my options. (One option really. Cash was out of the question.)

I could mount an expedition to some Malaysian or Central American rainforest and scrounge around for fallen branches to plunder -- no need to cut down a whole tree for one chair, after all. Then back home I'd mill the branches into boards, assemble the chair, teach myself to weave upholstery fabric, and learn to sew together seat cushions.

Allowing a few minutes here and there for unforseen calamities, I figured the three days I had until our anniversary would be more than enough to knock a chair together.

Getting to Honduras with the local airport socked in by tule fog was a problem. The overland route to Central America is exceeding long, especially on bald tires. Instead of mahogany, I opted for some less exotic domestic wood scraps culled from my personal collection heaped in the corners of our garage.

Without exact plans, the chair design became difficult. I fell back on some Adirondack Chair plans I'd unearthed during the workbench cleaning process. Adirondack is a native American term meaning "land of the ponderously heavy and yet extremely comfortable lawn furniture."

My first rickety attempt made me consider a movie career as a breakaway furniture builder. But on my next try, I "nailed it," so to speak. It was too heavy to cart into the house by myself so I dragged it out onto the lawn.

The riot of emotions on my wife's face when she first saw it was a moment to "chairish" forever. Her knees were so weak she had to sit down. Gingerly at first -- she must have remembered the bookcases -- and then with her full weight (which she wants you to know is "just right"). When her strength returned she suggested we leave her present in its present place -- outside, "to age naturally."

It's been there a year now. Our cats use it all the time as a perch for snoozing, so perhaps it is a Morris chair after all.

A Short History
of the
Shelf Realization Fellowship

The simple truth is: things expand to fill the space allocated to them. The reference library here at Clear Creek Ranch always has forty to fifty more volumes in its teetering stacks than there is space on the existing shelves.

There is plenty of room on the non-existing shelves -- those are the ones that are constantly in the planning stages, or under construction. But once assembled, they are soon crammed so tight with essential reading matter that even the ranch silverfish can't put together a decent snack. New stacks pop up overnight, like mushrooms, on the remaining floor space.

All the shelving units here at the ranch bear the mark of my distinctive style. Picasso-esque, someone once described it -- during his cubist period. All the pieces are there if you look long enough, they just don't always face in the right directions. Books and planks undulate precariously along the ranch house walls to the point where I often find myself pondering a variation of the old conundrum, "which came first, the books or the shelves?" (or which is holding up the other for that matter?).

The point of all this is that I wanted to improve my woodworking skills (which meant the massive purchase of new equipment) but I was short on cash. If I could form a cooperative venture with other like-minded folks we might pool our resources into something quite staggering indeed. But how to attract such kindred spirits?

An ad in the local newspaper yielded only one call, from a man whose compulsive do-it-yourself addiction had robbed him of family, friends, and funds. He was a recovering wood-aholic and a recent graduate of a twelve-step program (none of the steps built by him, he was proud to say), and his now-idle woodworking machinery was mine for a song.

Unfortunately I can't carry a tune in a bucket -- which I'd want to build first anyway. You know, one of those picturesque wooden wishing well-type buckets, just as soon as I can find the plans jammed in there somewhere on my bookshelves. But the idea was to swap things cooperatively, not to buy them outright, so I moved on.

To attract members I needed some kind of spin, a gimmick. I noticed that the most successful businesses in the little town near Clear Creek Ranch are specialized, and seem to have a New Age flavor about them -- east Indian mysticism, crystals, that sort of thing. Where could I fit in?

As Swami Drummond-anda, founder and guiding guru of the Shelf Realization Fellowship, that's where.

A few of my disciples showed up for the first meeting in flowing saffron-colored robes they'd fashioned from old bedsheets, but we decided that this would be dangerous around the machinery. Soon we were all sporting a more practical look: plaid shirts, short beards, and beer-bellies in imitation of that public television demigod of semi-fine woodworking, Norm Abrams. Our mantra: measure twice, cut once, and you're Om free.

We begin each session with a guided imagery meditation, focusing on some aspect of tool safety, such as the sound of one hand clapping. Which is all you might have after a major mishap with the table saw. Safety glasses are also required. Several of my followers had special ones made that include protection for their third eye.

We considered a suggestion to sprinkle crystals around our workplace, but when all the machinery is going we don't need any more vibrations. Smoldering incense in a room filled with flying sawdust also seemed too hazardous.

As guru, I worry about the future. So many of these organizations, founded with such high ideals become mired in conflict, in-fighting, charges of sexual harassment. I am pretty sure that couldn't happen here. Any verbal harassment will be drowned out by the din of the machinery, and anything more physical will be deterred by all the sharp implements within everybody's easy reach.

Our commune's dream now is to craft a permanent Om. We will pull the necessary permits as soon as the stars are properly auspicious. Which I won't know for sure until I find that astrology chart wedged somewhere in my library.

Trowel and Error

It all started when a sliver the size of a Cross Pen got stuck in my big toe. Not a remarkable event out here, except that I was sitting quietly in the reading room at the time.

You probably have such a room. It is small and quiet, stocked with stacks of reading material, towels, good lighting, seating accommodations for one, and is located close to a roll of perforated "notepaper" permanently mounted on the wall.

I tend to adjourn to this sacred perusal room on short notice, as the spirit moves me (or at least threatens to move part of me). Such is my haste that only rarely do I remember to bring my newly-required reading glasses with me. With advancing middle age my minimum focal point has moved too -- about twelve inches beyond my fingertips. Now I am forced to remove my shoes. The better to turn the pages of the sacred texts that arrive daily via government messenger from Eddie Bauer, L.L. Bean, and Victoria's Secret All-Flannel Edition.

It was while fast-forwarding through the down-filled teddy section that my big toe picked up the aforementioned sliver. Not from the catalog -- from the floor. You see we still "trod the boards" in our unfinished reading room -- subflooring holds center stage after all these years.

A rough-hewn profanity issued from my lips. "Hi ho sliver, away!" as I recall. It bounced around this acoustically-perfect chamber where I often yodel renditions of faintly-misremembered rock arias, and use the large mirror for practicing air guitar. And perhaps in the future, air sitar. For in this room of harmonic convergence I became a New Age Channel Person.

When my Spirit Guide introduced himself, it was a good thing I was sitting where I was. You could have knocked me over with a feather. One of his feathers actually, for my guide is a native American chap named Gray Water (no, not Tonto).

When I heard his name I surmised he was a water sign (or at least a waste water sign), an artisan, a builder of ancient aqueducts, a plumber, perhaps. But no, as I would learn, he was a pioneer electrician. Restroom related, to be sure -- around the turn of the century in Oklahoma, he had been the first Indian to wire a head for a reservation.

Any reservations I had about Gray Water were quickly

confirmed. Among his favorite phrases, something about "not judging a man until you've walked a mile in his tepee." At least I think it was tepee. Given the echo and the room I was in, it could have been something else. About this time I began to suspect that having lived in an earlier age didn't automatically make one sagacious.

Soon after my other-worldly visitation, I decided to tile the reading room floor. Rather than call in The Tile Guy, I decided to do the job myself. If Simon Rodia could build the Watts Towers singlehandedly, it would be small work to cover a 5'x9' room in tile. "It's such a little project, how long can it take?" I asked my wife. She rolled her eyes. We both knew I'd just sealed my fate better than I could ever seal the floor.

The tile showroom was aptly named Tile We Meet Again. My wife and I met with the salesperson a dozen times before deciding we couldn't decide on a single color. I opted for the "one of each" approach: one tile of every brand, color, size and shape. The floor and walls would soon be a riot of color, hopefully none of it my blood shade, as I didn't consult my wife first.

In addition, I incorporated some of my collectibles into the pattern. Casino dice, dominos, mahjongg tiles, old porcelain doll parts and all my obsolete Chuck & Di commemorative china. What better place for those royal squabblers than the Clear Creek Ranch throne room?

Proper tools make any job easier. Knee pads and prozac should top the amateur tilesetter's "required" list. Since each piece was unique, why use a straight edge or level? The result looked like a bad geometry example: a miniature world of colliding planes, each flat, yet slightly tilted.

A hard-won tilesetting tip: after smearing cement-like grout all over the tiles and working it into the cracks, do not wait until the next day to wipe the tiles clean. Unless you are trying to achieve a non-skid surface, that is.

After several weeks I finally stepped back to survey my artistry. The disembodied doll hands reached out to me. Their tiny unblinking eyes, stared down on me. What had I done? How could I ever read with them looking over my shoulder. I felt like throwing in the trowel. And I would have, if I hadn't already grouted it into the corner.

Protracted Mini-Contracting

Shortly before my sister had her first baby I spotted a tiny school desk at a yard sale. A little paint-stripping, sanding and refinishing, I thought, and it would make a cute addition to my new niece's room. This wasn't a high priority project, since the kid wouldn't even be sitting up for more than a year, so I set it aside for a while.

Since then, my sister had two more babies, the Vietnam War ended, Nixon left the White House in disgrace, and quite a bit of water has passed over the gate. And I am just about ready to start refinishing that little desk -- not that any of my nieces could fit into it now, but maybe one of their children can (if I start right away).

You see, I was born in April on what was supposed to be Saint Procrastinatus Day. The date was re-assigned to someone else when he didn't turn in his resume on time. Saint Procrastinatus is famous for saying "The canus ate my homework," which in his case was true. Would a Saint lie?

More importantly, do school kids sit in desks anymore? I understand they lounge around in study groups, clusters, cliques, cadres, triads, gaggles and pods waiting for the smart kid to come up with the right answer so they can all pass the course. But I bet some of them would still play with a dollhouse.

That's another project I have on a long-extinguished back burner. For decades now, I've been collecting just the right parts (and my thoughts) while the dollhouse plans have been collecting an impressive coating of dust.

At first the dollhouse was going to be a plain plywood structure: two stories, open back, maybe a real stairway, but probably not. A one weekend project, sturdy enough to last until the kids were tired of it -- hopefully covering more elapsed time than it took me to construct it.

But then remembered the school desk delay. To compensate for my desk-bound guilt, I gilded the dollhouse's simple boxy design. It became an elaborate exactly-to-scale Victorian facade -- fancy fretwork, gingerbread, tiny shingles. A detached combination stable/garage complete with servants quarters was added, because there was no way the tenants could keep up a place like this by themselves. Two stories became three, plus an attic to store crazy relatives in, and a basement/cellar for other family secrets.

To heighten the realism, I built a platform for "the grounds" surrounding the house. A tiny formal garden followed, with a central fountain, and of course a small pond, a gazebo, a greenhouse, and a potting shed. The whole thing would be surrounded by wrought iron gates and moss covered stone walls painstakingly fashioned from quarry gravel.

Initially the grass and the paths were going to be painted on. But then I recalled the many pleasant hours I'd spent mutilating and deforming shrubbery (my bonsai period -- when I pulled some impressive stunts), and I opted for living vegetation. Not real grass, but moss and other diminutive flora that would mimic its life-sized counterparts. I spent months combing the seed catalogs, and cruising every nursery within a day's drive of the Ranch.

Next I pondered the plumbing requirements for the garden fountain, and decided to run pipes into the main house as well. Two fully functioning water closets, hot and cold taps in the kitchen, and a claw-footed tub off the master bedroom. Same for the servants quarters (in these egalitarian days, they'd need a place to hose off occasionally too).

Then the dark chandelier in the ballroom screamed out for light, and I realized both the dumbwaiter and the birdcage "lift" that could be used in lieu of the spiral staircase would function more smoothly on an electric motor.

In keeping with my always-politically-correct philosophy I went with a self-sufficient energy generation system. The water supply is pumped from the pond into the dollhouse by a windmill (that faces an air conditioner), with waste water piped to leach lines that water the grounds. Electricity comes from a small solar collector mounted on the dollhouse roof. Any excess (about a kilowatt minute per every other month) is routed through the Ranch electrical system and sold back to the power company where it helps offset the cost of all the conversion hardware. (No break-even point in sight).

Furniture, drapes, wallpaper? I'll get around to that if the bank appraiser can justify a large enough second mortgage on my dollhouse. It's already worth more than the rest of Clear Creek Ranch. And that's right, mine. I'm not sure my nieces will ever be old enough for it.

Those 5:01 Blues

When I had a regular 9 to 5 job in the city, there was no time of day that I looked forward to with more anticipation than 5:01 PM, especially on Fridays, and even more so when those Fridays signaled the start of a three-day weekend -- a time of happy hours when my time was my own. It's funny how a simple move to the country can change one's perspective on the meaning of time.

Over the years since our rural move, working at home on my own schedule, I have learned to dread the sinister sweep of the minute hand as it approaches the five o'clock hour. For when it does, I know that everywhere around me folks are closing up shop and going home for the day and I must put up my guard and have my wits about me. You see, it is at 5:01 PM, often on Fridays, and always at the start of three-day weekends, that things begin to happen at my house: a shoelace breaks, a bulb burns out, a pipe bursts, the pump quits, the electricity vanishes, the chainsaw sputters, tires flatten, batteries go dead, the cat suddenly needs minor surgery at the vet's. And for the next three days, the only people who will be on the job when I call are answering service employees.

You think I am exaggerating, right? Well if I am, why did the labor pains start last year the minute the Memorial Day weekend got underway?

No, no. My wife didn't give birth. I did!

I'd just come in sore from an afternoon of weeding in the garden and had shucked my work clothes. I was well into the preliminary negotiations with my wife for a back rub, when the first twinge hit.

"It really hurts right here," I said, jabbing myself in small of my back. What had been a dull throbbing suddenly exploded into searing pain and I collapsed on the floor in a ball.

"You ought to be on the stage," my wife said. "That looks like it hurts. Very convincing."

I drooled on the rug and wondered if my life insurance was paid up. Visions of high school biology class flashed through my mind.

"What side is my appendix on?" I groaned.

"Your side, I hope," my wife said.

But when I didn't smile, clinching my teeth in a death-like rictus, she got the message and went for the phone. But the 5:01 syndrome was in effect: no one was in.

We had no family doctor. The only physician I knew lived 500 miles away and retired 20 years ago. My wife suggested the hospital emergency room, but a nurse friend of ours, a 20-year E.R. veteran, had filled my head with scenes of gore and bloody atrocities.

"No," I protested, "that's where the sick people are!"

"I think you qualify," she said.

I was too weak to argue. A body bag would have been more appropriate, but she helped me dress while I remained curled in a fetal position. Then she rolled me into the back of the truck, and we bumped down the road for an expensive evening in town. It was to be the first of many.

You see the "Stones" were on tour -- kidney stones, that is. These stones don't roll exactly, they have jagged edges. They cling and tear, every excruciating centimeter of the way. It wasn't long before I had my own cup down at the lab and I was gobbling pain pills like candy. While lying on a stainless steel table, surrounded by tubes and wires, I endured x-rays, injections, insertions and pyelograms in the name of science. The little stone crept slowly toward the open air.

And then one day, it all stopped as suddenly as it had started. Peace at last. The diagnosis was that the little guy had dissolved on his own. Which was fine with me. I'd read the Reader's Digest story entitled "I am Joe's Kidney Stone" (no kidding) and I wasn't looking forward to the last few inches of his travels.

That Friday I picked up a thick packet of mail from the mailbox and sorted through it. Fourteen inscrutable computer-generated bills from labs, urologists, radiologists, pharmacists, and people I'd nodded to in the hospital hallways. The totals were staggering.

I picked up the phone to straighten this thing out. But of course there was no answer. It was 5:01 PM.

Ab-solutely the Last Word on Abs

You may not be able to tell it by looking at me, but I do not have abs of steel. Trust me. None of my non-atrophied body parts even vaguely resemble any sort of metallic object.

The most that could be said for some of my muscles is that they are firm to the touch. But then so is Jell-O salad. Which is usually located in the kitchen next to those flimsy old tubular dinette chairs that some enterprising infomercial folks have cut up, bent, and reassembled as Abdominal Muscle Crunchers. Just three easy payments of $29.95 each.

Odds are your personal Ab Cruncher will be earmarked for the next garage sale before that third credit card payment is due. It is time to pen that letter of complaint to (who else?) Dear Abby. The ancient Abster will no doubt advise us that the world is divided into two camps: the Abs and the Ab-nots.

I like to think that the Abs are egocentric, elitist freaks of nature blessed with over-active metabolisms, and the Ab-nots are normal, flaccid, salt-of-the-earth types.

Actually, even the ab-nots have abdominal muscles. They just don't flaunt their existence in public. They also pack several extra layers of adipose tissue around their personal six pack as insurance that their intestines will stay in place. Spare tires serve a valuable purpose on your vehicle, why not above your belt buckle?

At my age, no amount of dieting and exercise is going to make me look like a member of the Olympic Men's Gymnastics Team. The washboard abs of my youth are taking on the shape of the washtub instead. And although I'm not too far gone (yet), I have quit wearing tight-fitting t-shirts in favor of loose-fitting Hawaiian shirts with the tails tucked out. As if I'm really fooling anyone into asking themselves, "Is all that under there his stomach, or just an atrociously loud shirt billowing out in the breeze?"

And speaking of metallic body parts, I used to possess a mind like a steel trap -- fast, sharp, unrelenting, remorseless, deadly. But lately my mind is acting more like one of those traps that snares animals humanely, without harming anything. Except in my mind's case, a spring is sprung somewhere and any ideas I may have captured are now free to wander off unsupervised.

In honor of my growing dementia, my wife (I think) got me a slogan shirt that says "If I could remember your name, I'd ask you where I left my car keys." I had to hold it out at arms length to read it because I couldn't find my glasses.

I don't have the heart to remind her that I no long wear shirts that tuck in. My plan is to tuck the shirt away in a drawer for a few weeks until we both forget about it, and then when I unearth it again, to give it back to her. I'm not being cheap, I'm recycling.

We recycle the reading material out here at the ranch too. Re-reading is another word for it, but that would mean we remember reading the book before. As a rule, we don't.
Mostly we read mystery novels. If a 3"x 5" bookmark is inside, I know that one of us has already read it. As we read we note down all the characters when they are introduced throughout the book. Otherwise by the time we reach the denouement 200 pages later, the main mystery would be "who are all these people What-his-name, the detective, is talking about?"

We don't take notes on Mickey Spillane novels, of course. He only wrote one book back in 1946 and has repackaged it every few months for the past fifty years with a newer, increasingly lurid cover.

And speaking of covers, it's about time to wrestle the lid off another gallon of my favorite workout compound. No matter how many scoops . . . I mean reps I do with this Heath Bar Crunch stuff, my well-padded abs never feel the burn.

Just Hanging Around

Everyone warned me that keeping up a place like Clear Creek Ranch was going to involve a lot of manual labor. My formerly desk-jockey hands had to be retrained immediately if I planned to do more than shuffle papers (a skill of little value out here in the woods). Paper cuts became a distant memory as my soft city hands were repeatedly pummeled, pounded, scraped, and bruised as I went about my new chores.

The term "back breaking" quickly moved from the category of "hyperbolic figure of speech" to one of throbbing reality. And where before I had often been accused of <u>being</u> a pain located near the lower end of the spinal column, now I constantly <u>felt</u> one -- among the many aches and twinges all the way north to my neck.

I tried a number of remedies, with limited success. My personal quest for relief took me through muscle relaxants, heating pads, ointments, Ace bandages, long soaks in the tub, stretching exercises, hatha yoga, chiropractic therapy, massage, acupressure, acupuncture, meditation, and prayer.

Along those spiritual lines I even tried a liberal application of organic wine to my internal organs under the misguided assumption that the name of the Greek wine god (Bacchus) sounded like he might have something to do with that part of the body. The resulting organic hangover, I am sad to report, wasn't worth the temporary relief.

"What about martial arts?" my wife said as she was kneading my tense trapezoids into submission one evening."

"I don't see how drawing pictures of cowboys is going to help," I grunted through pain-clinched teeth.

"Nor do I, my improperly-oriented one," she continued. "I was referring to judo, karate, tai chi chi'uan, et al. I hear it's excellent conditioning."

I pointed out that we'd just spent $50 overhauling the chainsaw, so there wasn't a screaming need to start karate-chopping logs into firewood. Then again, sore hands might take my mind off my sore back. And I'd always liked activities that can be performed in one's pajamas.

A new aikido school was forming in town, so I gave it a tumble -- literally. Although it is considered to be one of the more gentle martial arts, aikido still involves a lot of falling down (actually, rolling with the punches), as well as oriental lingo and a cosmic, quasi-spiritual aspect. I went through a few preliminary lessons in the dojo (practice hall) but I didn't get the immediate relief I was after.

"How did it go?" my wife asked as I unlocked the door.

"The dojo was working, it just didn't work on me," I said, putting my ki in my pocket.

Never one to be trendy, I checked out the Batman video for the first time recently and was intrigued by the scene where Batman was "relaxing" by hanging upside-down. Maybe if I hung by my heels it would stretch my aching back!

The next day I got a pair of Gravity Guidance Inversion Boots. Each "boot" is a padded metal cylinder with a hook on it. They strap around your ankles so you can safely dangle from a chin-up bar secured in a doorway. I used a sturdy bar already in place in my closet.

My first discovery was that I am not as limber as I used to be during my jungle gym days (circa 1953, age 6). The actor playing Batman who is about my age probably had two stagehands hoist him into position.

When I finally I kicked and squirmed myself into inverted position several gallons of blood immediately surged into the veins and capillaries on my face, and all my major internal organs tore loose and slid into my rib cage, firmly lodging somewhere in my throat. My entire head throbbed in time with my rapid heart beat.

My mind raced as I wondered just how grizzly I'd look by the time my wife discovered my body and the coroner dropped by to examine my remains.

"Did he hang out here often?" he would ask with a smirk.

Then, as I was formulating my wife's snappy reply, I heard something pop, again and again. Suddenly the painful tension in my spine was gone. My pulse slowed.

Sweet relief. Now all I had to do was get myself down off the bar . . . after completing the toughest sit-up of my life.

I wonder how much one of those stagehands costs?

Muscle & Fatness

You may have the impression that I exist in a constant state of turmoil and crisis, teeth gritted, neck veins popping, perspiration flowing in torrents, with gallons of adrenal secretions coursing through my body at any given moment. This is an understandable conclusion, given the numerous plots against my sanity and well-being that are hatched daily by the electrical appliances, wildlife, and inanimate objects around Clear Creek Ranch. I should be a lean, taut, tight, twitching bundle of nerves.

In reality, my middle-aged body is softening and could use some vigorous exercise. Arnold Schwarzenegger is about my age, and he still has some muscle tone, judging by his appearance in Terminator II -- the early scenes where the wardrobe department seems to have misplaced his costume. At least I assume he doesn't owe his muscles to the prop department.

I grabbed some "fitness" magazines from the newsstand, looking for tips on a quick fix -- a "one-minute-manager type" approach. But there were no articles entitled "How I Flattened My Stomach and Added Six Inches to My Biceps Using the Once-In-A-While-When-I-Feel-Like-It Workout."

What I found were long-winded articles about strict exercise and diet regimens that were exhausting to read, and pictures of grinning, glistening, massively meat-covered bodies in little tiny underwear with numbers on them. While I wanted to be fit and healthy, I'm wasn't ready to join a circus sideshow.

I flipped the magazine pages hoping for a shot of someone whose chest measurement wasn't three times the size of their waist. The math on that one required about 100 inches for me, which would take some doing even if I "cheated" a little and ran the measuring tape around the outside of my outstretched arms. I did find one shot of a bodybuilder who was flexing back muscles for the camera. The proportions seemed almost normal until I realized the subject was a woman, not a man. Well, if she could do it, so could I.

The first day of my new health regimen went smoothly. I broke into a mild sweat early as I assembled and bolted together the weight bench and unpacked the barbells and weights. Then I experimented with several alternative floor plans to come up with the best way to display my new exercise equipment in the corner of my office. It was time to hit the showers. No point in overextending myself. That could come later.

The weights were accompanied by a brochure with some basic exercises. These were illustrated by black and white line drawings of a musclebound Stallone-clone and the muscles being worked by each exercise were highlighted in blue, yellow, and red.

After the assembly session, I rested my muscles for about a week. Feeling energetic one morning, I followed the brochure's instructions and concentrated on my leg muscles, doing a variety of squats and leg lifts using light weights. Soon I began finding muscle-remnants I didn't remember having. The workout seemed so easy that I added more and more weight and did double the repetitions suggested for a novice.

My legs were tired and tingling as I showered. They gave out completely as I was drying off. I hit the floor, got up, and hit the floor again, and again. I could crawl -- that gave my upper body a mild workout -- but I couldn't walk for the rest of the day. Every time I tried, I landed in a heap, providing hours of amusement for my wife.

The aftermath of subsequent workouts was never as dramatic as that first day, and I have to admit that after several months of semi-regular use, my enthusiasm has waned. Mostly, the weight equipment sits in the corner unemployed.

"All that expensive equipment gathering dust," my wife sighs. "What a waste."

"Yes dear," I answer, sucking in my undisciplined waistline "but now that I'm 'in shape,' I can feather dust the whole thing without breathing hard.

Butt-kicking Memories

I came into the kitchen directly from the garden. I'd just spent an afternoon double-digging a couple of 10'x10' flowerbeds to the depth of one foot. The soil here at Clear Creek Ranch is full of clay. Digging in it during dry weather is like digging through a dense field of solid pottery. It is important to fluff it up with compost and organic matter if I expect anything to grow to normal size in it.

Don't ask me about the first carrots I planted. The packet showed long, slender beauties. What I got was dense, squat, marble-shaped mutants. Hardly worth all those weeks of weeding and watering. No hope of their contributing a fair share toward amortizing the costs of that protective six-foot deer fence I had installed.

On the way back from the garden, the accountant in me (my dark side) did the math as I dragged my shovel toward the shed. Double-digging moves a lot of earth. By completing two 10'x10' beds I'd dug the equivalent of a trench one foot deep and two hundred feet long, and then filled it up again!
Almost 15 cubic yards of earth -- a dumptruck full. Just me and my trusty, dusty shovel.

I was feeling proud and exhausted when I got inside. I unlaced my workboots and kicked them into the corner.

"I suppose you'd like me to kick your butt," my wife said.

"Yeah, that would feel great," I smiled in anticipation.

"Well, as much as you deserve it," she said eyeing the dirt clods and clumps of turf that tumbled out of my pants cuffs onto the carpet, "as much as you deserve it today, I have another idea. Here, read this."

Now most people reading the preceding verbal exchange would probably draw the following conclusions: 1) my wife is a husband-beater, 2) I (the masochistic beatee) enjoy a good pummelling, and 3) the paper she handed me was a divorce summons for getting the carpet dirty. Fortunately, most people would be wrong. Let me explain.

Ranch chores can be arduous. But with no resident masseuse on staff here, my wife and I routinely do the honors on each other's aching back and miscellaneous body parts. Kneading the needy, we call it. The problem is that while the needy one is relaxing, the kneader is getting tense. So then we reverse positions and try to work out those new knots, only to transfer the tension once again. After several such exchanges we are both so exhausted we barely have the energy to drop off to sleep.

My back muscles are the worst. They get tight and hard and ropelike. I've often said that what I really need is one of those petite oriental girl-masseuses to walk up and down my back.

"Not in this bedroom, you're not," my wife insists. "If your back needs massive foreign aid, there is only one type of tip-toer I won't veto."

Her idea of an appropriate masseuse is someone matronly, of sturdy peasant stock, possibly eastern-european, wearing a babushka, and with forearms a defensive lineman would be proud of -- ones she could break a vodka bottle over without wincing. In other words, built like the opera's proverbial fat lady. It (and I) certainly would be all over if someone like that ever folkdanced across my sacroiliac.

Professional arbitrators are as rare as lottery winnings out here at the ranch. We worked out our own compromise. I lay on my side and my barefoot wife sits facing my back. Using only her feet and leg muscles she quickly, and almost effortlessly, beats/kicks my rebellious back and thigh muscles into submission. It has become my regular request after a hard day in the fields.

And now she was serving me papers -- a book, actually. One about stretching. Dozens of ways to warm-up before exercising, or to release built-up muscular tension afterward.

I tried it a few times, and it does work. But it's not the same. I'm really going to miss getting my butt kicked.

No Sox in the Bedroom

After weeks of rappeling down the hillside to our spring and trudging back uphill with five gallon water buckets sloshing in each hand, then splitting stacks of knotty green firewood with a glorified sledgehammer, and finally double-digging our one acre garden by hand while spreading sixteen cubic yards of turkey droppings therein, I felt entitled to a backrub from my wife. What I got was a piece of paper -- a gift certificate to a local masseuse.

Now a lifetime of city living left me with only two masseuse images in my memory bank. One was of an old prizefighter who'd taken too many direct hits to his frontal lobe and was now legally blind. His domain was the massage table at the local Y, where he pounded out a living by relieving charlie-horses and popping backs into place. He certainly knew what he was doing. The only problem was he had all the finesse of someone wringing out a dish rag. The other image was of the Hollywood Blvd-type massage parlor, complete with high heels and severely-fitted lingerie (usually worn the masseuses, only rarely by the clients), and the strong possibility of illegal activities.

Happily, my wife's gift certificate was for neither, although I was still careful to stack my clothing so I could pick it up on the run if there was a police raid. I entered the room as gnarled and knotted as the hunchback of Notre Dame, and emerged an hour later as limber and supple as the dish rag I mentioned earlier. The only problem, the process was mildly addictive. I soon found that I needed daily sessions to maintain even a moderate a feeling of well-being, and frankly I couldn't afford it.

It didn't help that I live in one of the New Age meccas of northern California where masseuses are more plentiful than crack dealers on inner-city street corners. Temptation was everywhere. It seemed that my town's economy consisted of several hundred people, each with their own portable massage tables, walking door-to-door giving one another enlightened backrubs and passing around the same $20 bill.

Since a local massage school was cranking out graduates as fast as their tuition checks cleared, my wife and I decided to learn the basic moves for ourselves. I figured we'd break even after trading a few rubs with each other.

Our instructor told us to bring bathing suits and our checkbook. We met on a redwood deck strewn with mattresses and six other couples including one male-male and one female-female pair. Several of the guys looked like their wives had talked them into it, and everyone was staring at everyone else. There were more stretch-marks (on the guys) than I'd seen since my draft physical in the late '60s when you could get a 4-F for being overweight.

I decided then and there that I could never be a professional masseuse. I didn't want to touch (or be touched by) anyone else in the class except my wife. We all drenched ourselves in almond oil, slid through the basics in a few hours, and slipped on home poorer but enriched. After one try we decided not to use oil at home --- the only flat surface we have is our bed, and when we were finished the room smelled like an old tossed salad.

The most important thing we learned that day was foot reflexology. The simplified theory is that your big toe equals your head, your heel equals your hips, and the spots in between represent various internal organs normally housed between those two points higher up on your body. I don't know whether I believe all that, but I do know how good it can feel.

After a hard day on my feet, there is (almost) nothing better than lying on the bed and getting a good foot rub. Around Clear Creek Ranch, this activity is known as ecstacy without sox.

There's Always A Spot
At Our Dinner Table

I'm pretty sure we will never starve to death out here at Clear Creek Ranch. If things get too bad we can take the splattered clothing I wear to eat dinner and toss it into a pot of boiling water. In no time we'll have a full-bodied, flavorful soup stock. Plenty of good solid nutrition in all those leftovers accumulating on my shirt front.

Let me go on the record as saying that I didn't used to be a slob. Now most of my dining attire resembles a bad Jackson Pollock painting, which is to say it looks like a painter's drop cloth. Properly framed and mounted, some of my tee-shirts could be museum quality. Very colorful too. That green stuff is the pesto sauce. The red is marinara.

We eat a lot of pasta out here at the ranch, although neither of us is Italian. After decades of failed experiments, I finally figured how to prepare our pasta "al dente" -- that elusive state of pasta-ness between crunchy and mushy.

When we want "a change of paste" we call it by its German equivalent, noodles. Same dishes, different country -- our version of international cuisine. But whatever it's called, the sauce just doesn't stay on the food like it used to do. The phrase "aren't you a saucy one," has taken on new meaning as my favorite shirts become permanently freckled with the multi-colored multi-cultural evidence of my culinary preferences.

It's all part of the aging process, they tell me. Hearing loss, dimmed eyesight, diminished strength -- they have words of wisdom about all these signs of aging. Although I keep forgetting exactly who "they" are. "They" are also the ones who always notice when I get green leafy vegetables stuck between my teeth. That is embarrassing and reassuring at the same time. It means I've still got all my own teeth, which are mostly hidden behind my moustache, which in turn requires frequent raking and hosing down during mealtime.

Over the years we have tried all sorts of protective gear. A napkin tucked in the shirt collar picks up most of the falling debris, but at least one bit always eludes capture. Aprons display the same weakness although they are excellent for catching the really big stuff that hops off the fork for a dive into one's lap.

Garbage bags (clean ones of course!) with holes punched out for head and arms offered good protection, except for the sleeve areas. But everything tends to slip and slide off into puddles on the carpet. And garbage bags are uncomfortably warm, a trait they share with trench coats. Yes, we tried trench coats and they have much to recommend themselves: a dark, stain-hiding color, long absorbent sleeves, shoulder epaulets for stowing spare napkins, and a belted waist (easy to let out near the end of a satisfying meal).

The problem is the whole 1940's film noire atmosphere that the coats generate. We muttered secretively in code out of the sides of our mouths and were constantly interrupted as we glanced suspiciously over our shoulders. All our conversations began to sound like bad dialogue from a Mickey Spillane potboiler. Our appetites dwindled, but who could blame us? All our food was either black, or white, or some shade of grey. (I refuse to eat anything that Ted Turner has colorized).

I even fitted myself with a stiff plastic funnel-shaped device know as an "E" collar borrowed from the veterinarian's office. The problem was it was too funnel-like. Every slip between the fork and my lip ended up sinking inside my shirt.

Finally, figuring I could simply shower away the mess after dessert, I arrived at the table shirtless. The human physique can be a beautiful thing, I tried to tell myself with an affirmation-like chant. But beauty is subjective, and I was not the diner being subjected to the full impact of my naked splendor. My wife was.

"Please," she gagged, "I'm trying to eat over here."

So it's back to splattered shirts. Some evenings, my wife and I play a spirited game of connect-the-dots, or guess-the-mess, and simply ignore all these worrisome aging indicators. From the bibs of youth to the bibs of old age.

It only gets worse, they tell us. And it's when we begin getting a lot of unintentional spots on the inside of our clothes that we should really start to worry.

Having a Bad Hear Day

You would think I could understand my wife when she spoke to me across the kitchen table. It's fairly quiet out here at Clear Creek Ranch. But I am at an age where the occasional word is lost in the clink of silverware or the crinkle of newspapers.

Usually I get the gist of it even with a few words absent here and there. However there are times when I miss a crucial part of her topic sentence and nod along in agreement as she works her way through a lengthy paragraph, hearing every word she said, but not knowing what she is talking about.

If only we spoke in cartoon balloons, I could break eye contact for a moment and sneak a peek at the top line and ungarble those mysterious sounds. But most of the ranch house ceilings are too low to accommodate the balloon encasement required for long discussions.

Ah, the pleasures of middle age, when one's body begins to wear out, expand, and disintegrate all at once. And I am in denial. No glasses for me, no hearing aids, not yet -- I'm too young. I can see myself (but not too clearly in this light) being led into the optometrist's office for my first visit and answering "huh?" to every question.

Worse than not hearing something at all is to hear each sound correctly and yet still proceed merrily down the wrong path in homonyminous delusion.

My wife recently suggested that I write about "Heir Styles." That's what I heard. This seemed like an odd choice for my column but rather than ask a clarifying question, I dutifully pieced together an outline on cultural differences and how some folks were still having 18 or 20 offspring, while others had tapered off to 1 or 2 little scions upon which to pin all their genetic hopes. The result was unabashedly pedantic, only funny in 15 or 20 places, and clearly not what she had in mind.

"You didn't hear me correctly, oh wordy one," she said, repeating her suggested topic slowly.

I heard it with my own ears, and "Hare Stiles" did make sense: rural living, livestock, fences, and gates. The kind of thing I always write about. But I pride myself on only writing strictly from my own true experiences. Although we do have a bunny pasture -- two in fact, I have never constructed a stile (a device allowing humans to pass over or through fences while deterring the livestock from doing the same). When I pointed this out to her, she gave me a look that seemed to shout, "One of us is certainly hare-brained, oh lop-eared one."

She spelled it out for me, on a piece of paper this time: "Hair Styles." Of course!

I'd recently returned from a trip to town and described the large group ahead of me at the supermarket. Three generations of one family. Nice enough people, it seemed, although in something of a tonsorial time warp. Grandma with ponytail and bangs, balding grandpa with the vestiges of an early Elvis ducktail-waterfall coif, a middle-aged hippie son in tie-dyes and muttonchop sideburns (with a ponytail not unlike mom's), and his nose-ringed teenage daughter with spiky hair that looked like someone had been messing with the color control knob (only this wasn't TV).

There seems to be a point in everyone's life (usually in high school) when the comb stops experimenting and the question of parting being a sweet sorrow ceases to engage. What once was a living, growing statement of individuality, or peer conformity (or somehow, both), solidifies into some kind of humdrum helmet to help us butt our way through the day with a minimum of fuss and bother, and no decisions.

In twenty years time will we routinely see punk grandmas and skinhead grandpas? Nose rings on our bank presidents? Dreadlock-tressed brain surgeons?

Until then you'll find me hiding out here at the ranch trying to coax wisps of my thinning mane (essentially the same haircut since 1962) over that pesky bald spot that's slowly spreading on the back of my head.

Recent Apneans Here At The Ranch

Snoring is one of those things that is best done when one is alone. At least this is what I've been told. I must enjoy snoring, I do quite a bit of it when I'm relaxing, although I can't really say what gratification it gives me. To be honest, I've never even heard myself doing it.

There must be some connection between marriage and snoring, because as far as I can tell I never snored until I began sleeping with my wife. Here I am talking about sleeping-sleeping, not that other kind of sleeping which is really a delicate way of referring to another bedroom activity where the participants are anything but asleep during (at least in my experience anyway).

In the beginning I only snored when I slept in one half of the missionary position -- that is to say, flat on my back. After ten years of patient prodding by my wife's elbow I have been trained to sleep on my side. I try to accommodate her.

During the night as my downside deadened from lack of circulation I repeatedly awoke in pain. I shifted my upside down and downside up. Up here in the loft at Clear Creek Ranch this can be more difficult and noisy than it seems. In addition to the usual sheets and blankets, I am regularly covered with a thick sprinkling of domestic debris: housecats, TV Guide, magazines, VCR remote control, TV remote control, mystery novels, notepads, pencils, and bathrobes. (Come to think of it, that might not be snoring my wife allegedly hears, it could be cries of "Help, I'm suffocating under all of this!"

This shifting gives me some relief, temporarily. Aided by gravity my blood travels through me like the sand through an hourglass: steady, relentless, and in one direction. Soon it is all on the bottom again.

My wife thinks I should amend that hourglass reference to a three minute egg-timer, because that is about how often I shift from one side to the other. Apparently I flip over in bed and land the same way a fried egg "over hard" does. (Am I good egg? Are my thoughts scrambled? Is there a yoke in here anywhere?)

After several months of quiet sleeptime that consisted of nap-flip-nap-flip-nap-flip, my snore muscles somehow became reconditioned and rose to the occasion. In short, my wife awoke to discover that I could still snore a chainsaw-like aria, even while positionally-challenged. My wife's sleep-starved voice soon urged me to sleep on my stomach.

Sleeping while standing up, or standing on my head is more natural than sleeping on my stomach. The only one who likes to sleep on my stomach is the cat, during the winter. "If God meant for me to sleep on my stomach," I said, "She would have put my nose on the back of my head." I thought by using the female pronoun I'd make her smile.

"Perhaps I can help Her arrange that," my wife shrieked. She seems to be getting a little grumpy after losing all that sleep over the past 16 years.

Nights on my stomach, head twisted to one side, were followed by stiff-necked days when I was mistaken for an ancient Egyptian painter's model: pharaoh-like, body facing forward, head severely locked to one side. By noon I was usually able to rachet it free with a minimum of loud pops and screams. I rarely fainted.

But I soon continued my snoring. I tried wrapping a bandage around my head to keep my jaw shut tight. I didn't exactly snore after that, but I continued to breathe through my mouth. The ebb and flow of air rushing between my clenched teeth created a hiss that was really quite annoying. It even woke me up. On the plus side, I did not need to floss for the duration of this experiment.

We tried earplugs. They kept falling out of my wife's ears, and since I slept through my most bombastic arias, I sure didn't need them. Finally we decided on separate bedrooms. Unfortunately the only available sleeping area was another unwalled loft opposite ours.

"I can still hear you snoring," my wife said. "Only softer. It's eerie, like 'Mike's Ghost' is snoring. Besides, without you in bed, how am I going to keep my toes warm?"

How indeed. We are back in the same bed again and I'm doing my best. I probably won't snore at all tonight, I'll be manning the tape recorder. You see, last night during a sleepless moment, I think I heard a snore. Well, a petite snore-lette, and it didn't come from me. I want proof.

Perhaps soon we'll be performing nocturnal duets here at the ranch. Something to rival those coyotes out there on the hilltop.

Thanks For No Memories

There are many scenic distractions on the long, winding drive into town from my Clear Creek Ranch home: thundering waterfalls, distant snowcapped peaks, weed-filled auto graveyards. So many distractions that, if I don't have an errand list pinned to my shirt, I often forget why I am in town in the first place. I've been meaning to write about my failing memory for some time now, but the topic keeps slipping my mind.

Memory failure is often attributed to old age. As a teenager I used to know everything, and was not shy about sharing my wealth of knowledge with anyone within earshot. This irked my grandfather who also considered himself something of an authority on whatever topic was being discussed around the dinner table.

"Why I've forgotten more about (the topic I was expounding upon) than you'll ever know," he would often say.

At first I believed him -- after all he was older, and undoubtedly wiser. I began to doubt him when he repeated the statement during one of my youthful monologues on surfing. You see, Grandpa lived the first 75 years of his life as a farmer in a landlocked midwestern state.

Now, as I approach middle age, I see that Grandpa was making a statement that went beyond the topic at hand. It was a memorable statement about age, memory, and the powers of the human mind, although the exact words escape me at the moment.

Scientists claim we use only a tiny fraction of our mental capacity. Aerobic exercise leaders and other axiom-mongers urge us to "Use it or lose it." Paradoxically it is the tiny fraction of my mind that I have been using that I seem to be losing. Someone said that every time he learned something new, he forgot something old -- as if the mind were something with a fixed capacity. My brain works more like a swirling bottomless pit. Drop in a fact and it will eventually bubble to the surface, usually when it is too late to be useful.

Phone messages and important dates often fall into this category. Lucky for me, my wife's birthday falls on Christmas.

The big tree in the living room is a swell reminder. And as long as I get her at least two nice gifts (one for each event) she is happy. Although I still have trouble remembering her size. (For the record, it is either 8 or 18, which, I am told, is a very big difference. My life savings await anyone with a coherent explanation of women's dress sizes.)

Here's a memory trick I've learned. Recently I arrived in town to discover that I'd forgotten to pin on my list. I knew there were three errands to do for my wife, and one for me. Even though I'd written the list less that thirty minutes before, I couldn't remember any one of the four items. I tried an exercise based on Zen meditation, called "emptying." (A word of advice: don't try this while driving.) I closed my eyes, took a few deep breaths, and thought of nothing -- emptying my mind of the few thought-fragments that were wandering around in there. The theory is that this creates a vacuum and the lost thought I wanted would pop in.

Soon thoughts began to flood in and I quickly scribbled down one errant errand after another. When I stopped I had a list of twenty items. Very late that night I arrived home triumphant, with my completed checklist proudly pinned to my shirt like a first prize ribbon. While I ate a warmed-over supper (I'd forgotten to call to say I'd be late), my wife compared my zen list to the original list I'd forgotten under the magnet on the refrigerator door. None of the items matched. Not one of the items I did remember were needed.

"Still, I applaud your zen effort," she said, clapping one hand.

There are many books on memory improvement, but once I finally remember to buy them, they lay forgotten forever under the growing pile on the coffee table.

I was leafing through the community college's course offerings that arrived in the mail yesterday with the seed catalogues.

"Want to take a memory enhancement seminar, dear?" I called out.

"Night classes? Forget it."

"Forget what?" I asked.

Welcome, Out House is Your House

Today the subject is hygienics without hysterics. Proper bathroom etiquette, to be exact -- an indelicate area rarely explored by that Ms Manners person. Odd, since this is the one room that every member of the household needs to use everyday (usually at the same exact moment). The disputes that originate in the throne room have long been the basis of many domestic cliches.

Some examples: How does one properly squeeze a toothpaste tube? (Answer: from the end, neatly flattened and tightly rolled). Does the toothpaste cap belong on or off. (Answer: on. Until Colgate markets a fine wine, there is no need to allow its products to "breathe" before using). Is toilet paper best dispensed with an overhand or underhand delivery? (I must side with the over-the-top crowd).

Of course, I'm only expressing the <u>correct</u> way to do these things. How you choose to mangle civilized traditions in the privacy of <u>your</u> squalid abode is entirely up to you.

My formative years were spent in close proximity to a variety of female entities: my mother, aunts, and sister. After years of needling, I was trained to lower the toilet seat when I was done "doing whatever disgusting thing it is that males feel they must do with the seat raised."

However, I have observed that women, as a class, never lower the toilet seat lid. This would seem like a small thing to quibble about if I were not called upon by this same class of person to fish out barehanded so many small things that inadvertently splash-down where they don't belong. Things like earrings, hair brushes, bath towels, and since I am a vigorous tooth scrubber myself . . . my own toothbrush.

Which naturally brings to mind my brushes with house guests. House guests, like mosquitoes, are a seasonal affliction out here at the Ranch. The rare ones check into a motel, stand us to a dinner in town, bid us an early good night, and are but a pleasant memory by dawn. Others encamp long enough to justify jacking their encircled vehicles up on blocks and filing a change-of-address with the post office.

The matter of guest towel usage at Clear Creek Ranch is a moot, or rather moat, point. In my rather rich fantasy life (if not in reality) whenever we see visitors approaching we would raise the drawbridge. Some hardy souls actually swim the moat, at which point I hand them one of our own towels to dab moat juice from their forelocks.

Of course I have the good breeding not to mention where that particular towel may have been christened. Likewise with my vast supply of complimentary toothbrushes. Or for that matter, the fact that the moat is filled with irrigation ditch water that passed through miles of pasture and barnyards to acquire the proper level of murkiness.

It is with these unwanted visitors that a strictly enforced code of bathroom etiquette would allow me (in my dreams, at least) to conserve the contents of the ranch pantry and most of what I like to call my sanity. This would work best with lifelong city dwellers who have no idea where their tap water came from, or where it is going once it disappears down the drain.

At the first sign of urban interlopers I would shut off all indoor plumbing, post our "Throne Out At Home" sign, and activate the crude backup system we are forced to use during extended power outages. System is perhaps too grand a word. We unlock drafty shed, located 50 yards downhill and downwind, that houses our single hole, self-composting toilet.

As they are blotting the last of the moat goo from their persons, I would recite the Clear Creek Ranch composting toilet rules: No smoking out there! Only one kind of butt is permitted anywhere near the business end of our sensitive, 90's kinda plumbing. No foreign matter of any kind -- diapers, tarpaulins, or other feminine hygiene devices, etc.

Then I explain our septic system that digests disgusting waste products and distributes the resulting festering nutrients to those excessively green patches out there on the lawn. Which reminds me to warn them not to eat the fruit from the apple tree that is twice as big as any of its neighbors. Its root system, I explain, has tapped into the leach lines, and while things may look good, that fruit tree is doing the herbal equivalent of mainlining sewage.

If our guests do stay through dinner, almost no one has the apple pie (ala commode) for dessert.

All About Eaves

Our uphill neighbor recently tied into the county irrigation system. He always had enough well water for his house and garden, so this project was a luxury and not a necessity. His ponds, however, used to dry up by the 4th of July. They were built on the same Little Clear Creek that lends its name to our ranch. The mighty headwaters of our mutual creek only dribbles during the rainy season.

He tried to explain all this water delivery business to me: the months of cajoling and begging easements; surveying the best route for the pipeline; four inch pipe versus some other diameter; and, of course miner's inches. A miner's inch is an archaic measurement of water flow. It is the amount of water that can flow through a certain size hole, during a certain period of time, assuming a certain amount of "head."

Assuming you have a head for figures, you can work all this out on your personal computer spreadsheet, or you can take my word for it that a miners inch is worth a little more than eleven gallons a minute in this neck of the woods. Which appears to be about a gallon a minute more than my neighbor can use.

The excess economically trickles down into my pond, where the native frog population is rather jubilant, judging from the racket the bullfrogs make each night.

This new water pleases me as well. In summers-past my wife and I would walk out on the upstairs balcony in the morning to gaze upon our rural estate. In one direction, a verdant organic garden in full bloom. If we listened closely we could hear ravenous cutworms decimating our newly planted seedlings.

In the other direction was the parched hole that we called a pond in wintertime. Nervous frogs in ever decreasing numbers cringed in clusters around the rapidly shrinking circle of murky water in the pond's center. If we listened closely we could hear them croaking a blues version of "It's a Small World, Isn't It?"

Now that pond is full, crystal-clear to its 20 foot depth, and ringed by lush vegetation. We should be enjoying that view.

But we can't. The rain gutters won't let us.

We can see our rain gutters from our balcony. These are really sturdy, deep gutters -- six inchers. But they are a bit of an eyesore. They have accumulated all sorts of things over the years, mostly oak leaves and pine needles. I've never cleaned them out.

You see, I keep planning to adjust the gutters during the dry season so they will be "self-cleaning" during the rainy season. The force of the flowing water could theoretically push the dirt down the spout. So far I've been in the planning stage for about 40 seasons. I even have plans for secondary rain gutters to be installed below the originals, just to handle the overflow.

The original leaves have long since decayed, as have many successive layers. At this point we don't have rain gutters so much as we have several thirty foot long, six inch deep compost bins. In some parts of the world it would be considered prime farm land. Generations of field mice have called our gutters home. Our midsummer's eaves are alive with self-sown wildflowers and weeds.

My wife wants me to scramble up my old nemesis, the extension ladder, to give all this dirt the old heave-ho. I, on the other hand am lobbying for a new eave hoe. I'm considering planting carrots in our hanging gardens now. I'll probably just toss the seeds on the roof and let them roll down into the gutter. It won't be neat, but then why should the Clear Creek Ranch gutters be different from anything else around here.

I'd thought about other crops: overhead watermelons seem dangerous; strawberries would be nice, but the birds are less likely to go after root crops.

And those roots will help prevent soil erosion. At last, an ecologically sound reason to stay off that shaky ladder.
Let's call this strategy Clear Creek Ranch Climb-it Control.

How My Dam Vacation Eroded Away

For the past few years ditch water from the local irrigation district has been running through what passes for a creek out here. This is good for the frogs and the cattails and not-so-good for what was once the Clear Creek Ranch Seasonal Pond.

In its pre-irrigation water days, the pond existed only during the winter rainy season. During the summer the water evaporated, leaving behind a few desperate-looking frogs and a thirty-foot deep bone-dry crater. The red dirt that made up the earthen dam and equally earthen spillway hardened into dense, shovel-bending terra cotta.

Very little erosion occurred -- until the ditch water arrived. Now the pond is full almost all the time, and the tiny gallon-a-minute trickle of late summer is etching an ever-deepening canyon through our once-smooth spillway.

Last year, trying to maintain a semi-natural look along the creek bed with a minimum cash outlay, I covered the spillway loosely with native stone. The first good rain washed my handiwork downstream. Cement was the only answer. Lots of cement. The problem was getting a cement mixer down to the dam on our narrow, overgrown service road, and then pouring the concrete while the creek was still flowing.

Luckily the irrigation district turns off its spigot before the rainy season starts. This "window of opportunity" as my wife called it, coincided with the week I had designated as my "do nothing" vacation time. But how long could it take to hand-mix a few bags of concrete and spread it on the spillway, anyway? A few hours, one day at the most. Well maybe on one of those tightly-edited home handyman television shows hosted by some annoyingly cheerful guy in Dockers.

Early the next morning I drove into town for a few sacks of ready-mixed concrete from the do-it-yourself shop. All I had to do was mix in some water once I got home, but not until after I loaded all those 60-pound bags onto my little ½-ton pickup truck. I cinched up my back brace (these days I wear it when I pick up anything heavier than my wallet -- no chance of a back strain there) and went to work.

I figured about twenty bags would do the job, and although 1,200 pounds was a little over my new truck's load limit, I wanted to haul it all at once to save an extra 1½ hour round trip from the Ranch. Along about fifteen sacks though, the rear tires were flattening and the bumper was dangerously close to ground.

My only previous mixing experience had been with bread dough. The stuff would probably fluff up a bit when I added water, so I figured that fifteen might be enough.

Back at the ranch I decided not to ruin the paint job on my new truck by driving through the chaparral, and transferred everything into my rusted-out ranch truck.

Once on the dam, I stacked the bags next to the spillway, which was looking a lot wider than I remembered. As I broke for lunch a little quick math told me I'd just lifted a ton-and-a-half of dead weight and was still a long way from my do-nothing vacation.

All afternoon, I methodically lifted each 60 pound sack again and enthusiastically hand-mixed it in the wheelbarrow. When the last sack was empty, exactly half the spillway and nearly all of me was covered with cement. Water causes some things to shrink, I thought, and ready-mixed concrete apparently is one of them. The sun was sinking in the west.

Other than rescuing a tiny frog that hopped into the wet cement, the second day of my vacation was a chiseled-in-stone replica of the first. By day's end I'd lifted four tons of ready-mix to get only one ton on the spillway. I stood on the dam with my wife surveying my handiwork as I silently wondered if my cement-smeared work clothes would harden before I got back to the house.

It was then that she noticed how overgrown the cattails were getting and I sensed the eminent erosion of some more of my vacation time. She suggested that we/I dig out a few before the water rose and submerged their roots again. And then there was that new sandy sediment deposited at the upper end of the pond. We/I really ought to cart some of that up to fill in some of the low spots on the road.

"Sure," I agreed. "We/I only have a few more days of my vacation left, but how long could a couple of simple chores like that take, anyway?"

Lofty Thoughts

My wife and I may be the only people in the world who wear orange hardhats to bed strictly for safety reasons. About once a week for the past seven years my bare skull has bashed into a wooden beam that is part of the low ceiling in the loft area we call our bedroom. The beam is about twelve inches square, and if my experiences are any indication, it is very hard to miss. Well, the beam used to be square. After seven years of direct hits, its edges are rounding a bit and I am developing some odd-looking furrows in my brow. I don't think this is what my Dad meant when he told me to "use my head."

Loft living, while rustic and quaint, is not for everyone. There are days when I doubt that it is for anyone without wings or a prehensile tail. The only access to our sleeping quarters is a vertical ladder which requires a minimum of two arms and two legs, quick wits, a superb sense of balance, resin bag for sweaty hands, safety net, special suction cup shoes, basic paratrooper training, and assorted Grade Five (or better) rock climbing skills.

On the other hand, a loft is a secure place, safe from acrophobic predators. Our cats love it. They perch purring for hours on the edge of the bed surveying the house below, pausing only to fall asleep, or to cough up a fresh hairball to drop on the unwary. When it is time to visit the veterinarian, they head for the loft where they know I will be forced to do a one-armed rapple down the wall once I corner them and they have locked their talons firmly into my shoulder.

Living with a loft requires the kind of strategic planning usually attributed to World Chess Champions. In our case, the only things up-ladder in the loft are the bed, some clothes, the telephone, and the television -- which, of course, we only use to watch the cultural programs that PBS chops up mercilessly with interminable pledge breaks.

Consider the awkward possibilities of loft-dwelling. Midnight snackers, the kitchen is eight feet down! Beer drinkers, there is no plumbing within a commercial break sprint! Sleepwalkers, don't even dream about that stroll!

Of course, as with any two-story home, I always remember something I need urgently on one floor as soon as I arrive there from the other floor -- where, of course, that thing is. The upper and lower steps of our loft ladder are always dangerously cluttered with things that need to be taken up or down by the next available climber.

After several months of laboriously carrying the laundry down the ladder, I lost my balance for a moment and the basket crashed to the floor. Now this may seem obvious to you, but I never thought about it until that day: laundry does not break. Guess how the laundry travels now. Getting the clean and folded stuff back up-ladder is another story. After my initial discovery, I tried tossing it up over the railing, but it landed in one of the hairballs the cats didn't have time to roll over the edge. After that lesson soaked in, I went back to hand-carrying things.

Now that we are middle aged (at least I am) I am planning for the future. It is hard to visualize me at age 75 still losing my balance on the ladder. An elevator seems a bit pretentious, and, unfortunately, a conventional stairway takes up too much room.

I looked into installing a spiral staircase, but due to space constraints, the only way that can work is if the stairs twist under the beam that supports the loft floor. Which in itself is okay,

although not exactly aesthetically pleasing. The real problem being there is no head clearance for anyone over five feet tall. And on a good day my wife and I each tower a whopping seven inches over that height. So unless I can talk my wife into traveling between floors on her knees, it looks like we will be wearing our hardhats on the stairs too.

I'm looking into alternatives, but I haven't made much headway.

12-Step Program for Felines

A stairway leading to the second floor of one's two-story home seems like a reasonable expectation. It doesn't sound like a decadent luxury unless one is an Olympic-class gymnast-in-training or some sort of grasping, spartan, Grade-5 rock climber.

We certainly are neither of these rarified types -- Olympic-class pebble kickers, maybe . . . but we share one housal feature with them. We have yet to acquire a traditional stairway to our second floor here at Clear Creek Ranch. And given the rustic nature of the place, we also have no escalator, elevator, or dumbwaiter to hasten our commute between levels.

What we do have is a sturdy ladder arrangement, that works just fine providing the climber is unencumbered, unimpaired, clear-headed, sure-footed, and totally focused. Try that in the middle of the night sometime!

We talk about installing a staircase -- usually after a scary slip or stumble -- and have racked up quite a bit of verbiage on the subject over the past ten years. But we are no closer to the reality of a staircase than we were at the beginning. Talk, it seems, is cheap -- a great deal cheaper than any known stairway contractor will agree to work.

Given our floor plan, spiral is the only shape a stairway can take. Building such an intricate construction is probably beyond the skills of the novice woodworker -- a lowly rung on the achievement ladder, but one that I have yet to reach. My plans always look good on paper, but something major always gets lost in the transition to timber and nails. Folded properly in the shape of a paper airplane, even my plans would only stand a fifty-fifty chance of making it upstairs.

There are several companies out there that, for a price, will ship a stairbuilding kit to me, F.O.B. (whatever those initials mean -- full of boards? foolish owner-builder?). But their styles aren't my version of rustic, or the sizes are too big, or they call for too large an element of risk (like requiring me to locate and plug in my electric drill).

We even looked into the Lapeyre Stair which is really a series of staggered half-treads, alternating right and left, with handrails.

It's steep slope was perfect, but it had an industrial feel to it. Too much like being at the factory, or in the hold of a ship. Besides, our cats wouldn't be able to use it.

And they are the reasons I'm still in the market for a solution. The Clear Creek Ranch housecats are 14 year-old sisters. As you may know, 14 translates into quite a few dog years. The exact number escapes me. But according to Dr Reichenbach's scale, 14 equates to exactly 76 cat years. Like many theories, such as converting fahrenheit to celsius, this one sounds arbitrary and more than a little wacky.

A one year-old cat's "age" equals a 15 year-old human. But a cat doesn't age as fast after that first year. Over time it averages out to about 6 "human years" per calendar year (I was going to say purr year, but my editor has threatened to pun-ish me if I abuse more than two puns per column). So whether our cats are 14, 76, or 210 really doesn't matter. They are beginning to have trouble making it up and down our widely-spaced stairs.

What is important is allowing the flatulent cat enjoying a nap on my face in our sleeping loft to make it downstairs unaided in the middle of a winter's night to that spot near the backdoor where the "digging and burying facilities" are located.

So a month ago I built the cats their own stairway, using a 4"x4" post and a series of wooden platforms that spiral around it at easy-to-climb six-inch intervals. Sort of a feline 12-step program. Unlike many of my building experiments, this one is solid. I know because I forgot it was there and walked into it in the dark the other night. I was not the one left standing.

So far the cats have sniffed disapprovingly at the base, and deposited a truly stupefying hairball on the uppermost platform, but to my knowledge, they haven't set paw on it.
I hate to see it go to waste. If they don't start using it soon, I guess I'll turn it into a hospice for some of our many terminally ill houseplants.

No, I don't know how old they are in plant-years.

Aromatherapy Fails Taste Test

The other day I melted down a perfectly good 3-quart Farberware saucepan on the kitchen stove. This is an annual occurrence here at Clear Creek Ranch. It was, as always, an unintentional but nevertheless predictable event. Like the tides, or the swallows returning to Capistrano, or the cows coming home to roost -- a cyclical cosmic happening.

And while those other natural wonders are perhaps inexplicable, our midwinter meltdowns are not. The truth is, as always, I just plain forgot about the pan after I turned on the burner -- left the house for two and a half hours.

Returned in time to release several dozen cubic yards of densely-packed pent-up acrid clouds of smoke from the kitchen door. Mount St. Helen? Only the lava flow was missing, but just barely. Stalagmites of molten metal hung the bottom of the saucepan. Metallic vapors mingled with the carbonized remains of what once was going to be my lunch.

Metallurgists smelt ore, fishermen catch smelt. I have smelt all of the above (except metallurgists) and take my word for it, all smelled better than our kitchen did that day. I opened the windows. I turned on the fan. Despite the rain and near-freezing temperatures outside, soon every door and window in the house was open, including those on the windward side of the house.

There was no escape. The smoke permeated everything permeable, which apparently includes my brain. Some of the haze certainly fogged up my thought patterns. For a while there I actually believed the puddles forming on the floor and carpet would draw attention away from horrible stench.

About that time my wife returned from a trip to town. Her nostrils flared as soon as she opened the car door. She never has to ask, "What's cookin'?" Her nose always knows. In seconds her super-sensitive olfactory equipment can easily isolate every ingredient in a twelve course meal.

I awaited my fate.

"I sense the senseless demise of another $35 saucepan," she quickly sniffed. And then as she handed me her shopping bag she added cheerfully, without even a tiny hint of sarcasm, "What wonderful timing!"

Her shopping bag was brimming with what looked like brightly colored compost -- old dry rosebuds, twigs, leaves, vetchs, herbs, beetlewings, hair-of-the-dog, and seedpods of all descriptions.

"Potpourri!" she announced.

"Is gesundheit the proper response?" I asked, and suggested that we stuff a few of the larger flowerheads up our noses before we went inside but she demurred. As she entered, she let out one thoroughly theatrical but mercifully short gasp of dismay before whirling around the house in a flurry of activity.

As you know, here at the ranch we are into alternative cures to things. Our motivation is partly ecological and partly economical. Organic stuff, no pesticides or aerosol sprays, window cleaner made from vinegar and water, that sort of thing.

Soon every flat surface in the house held a bowl or cup which in turn contained a helping of the aforementioned floral compost mixed with water.

"Is this aromatherapy?" I asked.

"Not yet."

A cast iron pan went on back burner in the kitchen and another on the woodstove. Soon the compost was simmering, releasing a strong but pleasant aroma that eventually (about a week later) masked my earlier disaster, and some rather strong competition from the catbox. The over-all effect was that of a florist shop dumpster on a warm day.

As the potpourri cooked, the flowers released colors into the water until it was a rich wine color which reminded us of borscht -- a beet-based soup. Yum! Soon a pot of that traditional eastern European dish was slowly cooking on the other back burner. The finished product looked almost identical.

As I ladled myself the first bowlful and floated a huge dollop of sour cream in the middle something must have distracted me. Which explains why I can now say with great authority that potpourri smells much better than it tastes.

What A Tangled Web We Weave

I have been buttoning my own shirts and tying my own shoes for years. I can shuffle cards like a Las Vegas blackjack dealer, and give a split-fingered Vulcan salute like Spock of StarTrek with ease. I regularly use an adding machine correctly without looking at the keys, and type accurately by touch with all ten fingers (except for those hard-to-reach special function keys). I always thread needles on the first try, once my eyes focus, and I can tweeze out splinters with the calm aplomb of a neurosurgeon.

None of this should be construed as bragging really, but simply as the background against which I serenely agreed to help my wife dress her waist-length tresses.

While I am no concert pianist, I am not digitally-challenged either. It would be a easy matter, I thought, to follow the instructions in the hairdressing booklet and turn her long straight mane into a braided masterpiece.

After all, I routinely won first prize for weaving the longest lanyard at summer camp. As a former Boy Scout I could splice rope and tie knots with the ease of an accomplished sailor. However my language soon was peppered with phrases that were more naughty than nautical. Or since we were attempting a variation on the French Braid, perhaps I should say, "Pardon my French."

The French Braid is one step beyond the simple ponytail-divided-into-three-sections-and-plaited-together. The objective is keep adding hair to each section as it is braided, and (unless specifically agreed upon otherwise in advance by all parties) to end up with a straight and even construction on the back of the subject's head.

There should be a special uncomfortable place in the afterlife for those who write and illustrate "How-To" booklets on any subject. The pictures are so alluring, the instructional sentences so simple, and yet so completely impossible to implement -- such utter gibberish.

The booklet model's face is positively beatific as she illustrates the various steps in the process. It is my opinion that she is either thoroughly sedated, has had a radical lobotomy, or she is beaming in anticipation of the vast sums of money she will be paid for her role in this ruse.

A single tip for those who will ignore the hard-won secrets I am about to divulge: read through all the instruction steps <u>before you begin</u>.

This will ensure that you have absolutely no excuse for not having, for example, a "coated elastic" to hold the whole winding, lumpy mess together when you finally get to the bottom of things. We had several in a drawer in another room. This wouldn't have been a problem if both my wife's hands and the big toe on my left foot weren't irretrievably woven into the pattern of the almost finished Gordian knot on the back of her neck.

Other useful implements to have on hand: Valium, a gag, a bullet to bite on, assorted clips and clamps, and an extra pair of hands (without opinions of their own, thanks).

I've also found that the kitchen drawers offer help. One of those flat plastic spaghetti-sizers with various sized holes are ideal for dividing the hair into thirds. (Be sure to remove it <u>before</u> you actually begin the braiding process!).

Remember that it takes two to tangle and that snarls are best removed with a hairbrush, so make sure none of them are emanating from your mouth. The snarls, that is. You may actually need to clench the hairbrush in your teeth on occasion if your mouth isn't already occupied holding that pesky third strand.

Don't expect perfection on the first try. But do take a break before the whole thing degenerates into a frizzy Rastafarian dreadlocked nightmare, or the divorce lawyers smell blood and begin circling in a feeding frenzy.

And if defeat should come, as it probably will, accept it gracefully. Invest in a wig. I did, to cover those patches on my head where I'd torn out large hunks of my own hair in frustration.

Nobody here at Clear Creek Ranch will be guest starring on the Braiding Bunch Reunion Show anytime soon.

The Good, The Bad,
and
the Scrambled

"I could really go for some poached eggs with Hollandaise sauce on top," my wife said one sunny Sunday morning here at Clear Creek Ranch.

"Well, you'll have to go about 20 miles for them," I said. "Because that's how far it is to the nearest restaurant. And the nearest supermarket is a half mile beyond that."

"With gasoline costs and all, those would be pretty expensive eggs," she cheeped. "Wouldn't it be nice if we grew our own eggs right here at home?"

Grew our own eggs? Her choice of verbs gives you a barnyard idea of our combined knowledge in the area of animal husband-and-wifery.

Only a month before we'd heard a "joke" about a potato farmer who decided to go into the chicken raising business. For three weeks running he bought all the baby chicks available at the local feed store. On the third visit the store owner asked the farmer why he kept buying more chicks. The farmer shrugged and said that he just couldn't get the hang of it.

"I guess I planted the first batch too deep and the second batch too close together," he said.

I didn't get it. In fact I sympathized with the guy. I have the same problem with carrot seeds every year.

Still, the idea of readily available eggs seemed attractive. We got a book "Chicken Raising for Dumb Clucks" which we never cracked open, and went shopping at a used chicken lot not far from the Ranch. We felt that "mature" chickens would adjust to new surroundings better than baby chicks, which of course we had no place to plant anyway, what with all my experimental carrot patches taking up most of the garden.

Not wishing to put all our eggs in one basket, we got two pair of five year old New England chickens that the smiling salesman said were from Rhode Island and Plymouth Rock, although they were so obnoxious at first that they must have spent their formative years on the streets of New York City. I half-expected hard-boiled eggs.

Not that your average five year-old chicken lays many eggs to begin with.

"Can't get much toothpaste out of a tube that's been squozen every day for five years," my toothless know-it-all-after-the-fact neighbor said. "Too many miles on the old ovaries at that age. Best thing to do with those babies is pluck 'em and fry 'em up for supper."

"We're vegetarians," I said, trying not to use fowl language.

"Well, my supper then," he said hopefully.

The chickens became nobody's supper. How could anyone eat something with a name? And we had given them all egg-citing names: Shelley, Yoke-o, Henrietta, and Kiev. Poultry-geist was a name I suggested, but it didn't have a ghost of a chance. We turned our semi-retired egg-layers loose to haunt the garden and to scratch around eating bugs.

"Bugs are a valuable source of protein," I crowed.

"Uk," said my wife. "I'll remind you of that the next time one shows up in the salad."

Which is about all we can afford to eat here at Clear Creek Ranch nowadays. This chicken proposition has expanded like some government-mandated works project. There are department of housing costs (henhouse construction, insulation, running water, electricity, ventilation, cleaning); department of defense costs (police protection from skunks and other varmints); department of health costs (veterinary care); a staff nutritionist to make sure our guests' diet is up to scratch; and an employer-paid mandatory retirement package that amounts to more than chicken feed.

And what do we get in return? Again, it's a lot like most government programs. That's right, after all the squawking and ruffled feathers, we here at Clear Creek Ranch are feeling henpecked, with nothing much to show for it but a big goose egg.

An Irrational Fear of Moths?

I knitted my brow in alarm when my wife dragged a spinning wheel into the living room and announced it was time we started "growing" our own sweaters. I had long been aware that genetic engineering was capable of many odd things, such as the "geep," a goat-sheep-cross being, which you'd think could also be called a "shoat," but of course it can't because a certain style of pig already has that name. But I must have missed the news that the L.L.Bean catalog also had been crossed with a wool-bearer.

"Where do we purchase a packet of cardigan seeds?" I asked. "And how about a little argyle sock bush for over by the roses?"

"Very funny. I got a great deal on this fully-functional spinning wheel at the antique store and now all we need is some sheep."

"To spin the wheel?"

"For wool. They graze in our pasture and get all hairy, we give 'em a buzz cut, spin it into yarn and knit things for free. The simple life, back to basics, what could be easier?"

What could be easier . . . those words rank up there with "it'll only take a minute" on the Clear Creek Ranch Jinx-o-meter and pantheon of ominous sayings.

"What could be easier?" she repeated.

I thought about saying "A credit card, an 800 number and the Eddie Bauer catalog," but her heart seemed so set on this. "Okay," I said.

"Great, they arrive in the morning."

"They" were three sheep, a mother and her two yearling daughters. Ewe-y, Dewey, and Louise. If I counted them, I fell asleep (it doesn't take much). They were "loaners" from a neighbor down the road. We may be slow learners out here, but after buying a henhouse full of non-laying octogenarian chickens (who are still living in comfortable retirement out behind the garden), we decided livestock ownership was not for us.

Temporary sheep. An outright purchase would mean a lifetime commitment. With my luck we'd get some bald or naturally hairless variety with large appetites. Speaking of which, as vegetarians, if they were hairless we couldn't hack them up into lambchops. And would probably spend a fortune on sunscreen ointments and warm-up jackets for them.

No such problems with these sheep. Very wooly. Remembering drawerfuls of ruined sweaters I developed irrational fears about moths.

On the rainy afternoons when they grazed on high end of the pasture it was like a snapshot out of a British Isles travelogue. I had to fight the urge to don tweed coat and knickers and have a spot of tea before dashing off for the constable or the vicar or the village pub or something.

My wife wanted to get a Border Collie to help us round them up. Border collies are very intelligent dogs, smart and quick.

"If you want something around the house that weighs 40 pounds and is smarter than either of us," I said, "why not take in one of those precocious child TV actors? It would be annoying, but at least it could help out on the rent."

Whenever I need to herd my flock around I tie a halter to "mom" and the others follow along, like sheep. The cord is my shepherd, I babbled biblically.

A bag of sheared wool does not look much different from a bag of barbershop sweepings. It's a toss up as to which smells worse. Eventually ours got washed, dried, carded, teased, tickled, spanked, and ready for spinning.

My wife and I each took a turn at pumping the treadle to spin the wheel and pull the yarn. My calves (on my legs, we have no cows) locked up after an hour. I was sore for a week. It is no wonder pioneer people died so young, they were worn out. Rest in Peace (emphasis on <u>Rest</u>).

But not me! I'm busy now rigging up our stationary exercise bike to power the spinning wheel. Now one of us peddles while the other spins. Simplicity? We've logged enough miles to go to New Zealand and back and have quite a bit of homespun yarn but no new sweaters. My wife is talking about weaving now. A loom may loom on our horizon.

But as usual, we here at Clear Creek Ranch have yet to tend to our knitting.

Getting My Goat

"What do you think of kids?"

"They can be entertaining when viewed from a distance."

"What if we had a few?"

"A few? Even <u>one</u> would be more than we could handle at this stage of our lives. Besides, the bunkhouse here at Clear Creek Ranch isn't kid-proofed."

"Well I didn't plan on them coming inside. We could keep them out in the pasture beyond the picket fence."

So went a recent conversation between a certain Aries (Ram symbol) male and Capricorn (Goat symbol) female. The kids under discussion were of the four-hoofed variety, little goatlets. We were consuming vast amounts of cheese here on the Ranch, and much of it came from goat's milk -- feta cheese.

Feta is an acquired taste. It is a soft white cheese that often smells like it did time in a gym locker among the sweat socks, but tastes great.

"Don't goats eat a lot?"

"Sure, but they eat everything. Poison oak, weeds, you name it."

Neither of us thought to name the weatherstripping on our windows and doors, or all the blossoming tree branches in our orchard, or the practically-heirloom philodendron that has spread everywhere just inside the kitchen door.

The neighborhood goat-herdess, Cheese Louise, didn't bother to mention what compulsive browsers goats could be. Or what proficient escape artists.

Our wooden pasture fence, each post hole of which was dug by hand, by me, at a great personal cost of blood, blisters, and tears, proved to be no barrier at all. The goats either slithered under it like snakes, or boinged over it like kangaroos.

Soon little goats were gamboling on the deck, staring in as we ate dinner. Goats were in the flowerbeds, demolishing the few rose bushes that the deer had overlooked. Goats were on the freshly-painted hood of my sports car doing a tap dance that would have made that old hoofer Sammy Davis proud.

"Try to think about all the milk and cheese we'll be getting," my wife suggested.

"Yeah, when do we start getting cheese?" I asked.

"Just as soon as you hunker down there and start milking, my dear old goat," came the reply.

"But that means touching unfamiliar breasts -- animal breasts to be sure -- but breasts nonetheless. Surely this is woman's work."

Maybe somewhere else, but not at Clear Creek Ranch.

Getting the goat to stand still over the pail is an art I refuse to believe anyone has ever mastered. Nor can I believe anyone gets down on knees and elbows to milk a goat. I remembered, and was able to locate, plans for a goat milking stand in one of the cartons of woodworking project plans I'd purchased over the years.

Conceptually, the stand looks like a coffee table with a guillotine tower attached to one end. The goat stands on the table and sticks her head into the guillotine and eats whatever she can reach while I milk her.

The table worked fine, but the goat didn't. No milk.

"First ya gotta breed her," said Cheese Louise.

"Sex and feta cheese are related?" I asked.

"How disgusting," my wife added.

"You have to wait about four days after the kid is born," Louise said.

"What kid?" I cried, remembering my sports car. "No more goats!"

"Well, if she's not a mama, there ain't no milk."

"You mean we're taking the baby's milk?" my wife asked.

"Couldn't we share it?" I suggested.

Louise rolled her eyes. "That's not the way it's done."

We learned how "it" was done and where little kids go. Soon after that we swore off dairy products as a result. Although I do backslide when ice cream wanders by.

We switched over to a vegetable-based "soy cheese" that tastes about the same. But I'm never asking anyone how they get milk out of those little beans.

98

I Stink, Therefore I Am

Space is a valuable commodity here at Clear Creek Ranch. So when we needed more pantry space to store our growing collection of Mason jars, we did not scout the multiple listing services, or contact an architect to add on another wing. We (I) simply (some say crudely) put shelving up in an unused space under the stairwell.

The stairwell, unfortunately, is not attached to the house, but is part of our two-story garage that houses our "office" where these words are often written. And yes, of course, the ground level is used for vehicle storage. All is not topsy-turvy here. Our stairwell pantry worked perfectly and doubled as a drying room for the wide variety of herbs that grew like weeds (or at least among the weeds) in our garden. Hundreds of cone-shaped bundles hung from the slanting ceiling.

One evening after my wife finished the long mysterious shower that included "the ritual of the washing of her hair" she expressed a craving for salsa and chips. Well, my famous Scoot-on-the-Rug salsa is stored in jars behind a lead shield in the garage pantry.

"That old excuse, 'I just washed my feet and I can't do a thing with them,' isn't going to work this time," I said, holding the kitchen door open for her. "But I'll get out the power tools and start prying open a bag of chips while you're gone."

"My hero."

I had barely secured the chip bag in the vise when she flew through the door, jarless and jarred.

"I've been skunked!" she cried.

The odor rolled over me like a shock wave and I lost my balance. The chip bag burst open spontaneously.

"When I switched on the pantry light, there it was in black and white. I startled the little guy and he skunked me!"

99

"Clothes pin, dear?" I said, politely allowing her to attach hers before I clamped mine over my own twitching nostrils.

"What a great opportunity to utilize my vast and expensive reference library on foothill flora and fauna!" I thought.

"Leds loog ub an anny-dode," is what I said.

We soon determined that she had encountered a striped skunk, which as she just discovered, is a nocturnal animal.

"Spotted skunks are real skunks," I said authoritatively. "Your striped skunk is not a true skunk, it is a type of weasel. Minks, also in the weasel family, are said to have the worst odor. So you were lucky."

"I'm so relieved," my wife said through the fumes. "Enough anecdotes, let's have an antidote."

The 1903 edition Andersch Brothers' Camping & Field Guide suggested soaking in gasoline, rinsing in moist sawdust, and using chloride of lime to get rid of the odor.

"I'm not turning myself into a science project over this!" she said.

"Okay, there's more. Hang outdoors in the fresh air for several days. Burial should be used as a last resort," I read. "Oh wait, I've been reading about clothing odor."

Tar soap and tomato juice baths were among the remedies suggested. Several showers, shampoos and many open windows later the smell began to fade, but not the memory. Neither of us make many forays into the pantry now, especially after dark.

Our striped friend's visit has made a lasting impact in our kitchen as well. It seems our dangling herb supply absorbed some of his oily scent. Clear Creek cuisine has become more distinctive as a result.

It's not distasteful, just subtly different. Different enough to remind us of the time we now call "The Rise and Fall of the First Reek."

And They Call My Stove Chihuahua

Everything died in the garden last night, and for once I can't claim credit. If it wasn't already canned or sealed in plastic it never will be. Frost on the ground, freezing temperatures -- fall has fell. It is time to winterize the "manor house" here at Clear Creek Ranch. Time to cock the caulking gun and run a bead of something gooey around every orifice in the place. Weatherstripping, they call it. A cold war plot, I say.

My lips will turn blue in my frigid office while I try to type this column wearing two sets of mittens over my typing finger. My driving gloves are warmer and more convenient, but they are in my truck and the lock on the door tends to freeze-up this time of year. Yes, for the next month, as the thermometer drops, I will go into what is popularly known as "denial."

"It is not really cold," I will say. "We don't really need to build a fire yet, I don't need to haul wood, the cat's tongue is not really stuck to her drinking bowl."

I will muse for hours about the best was to phrase a joke with the punch line "I thought I thawed a pussy cat."

"Tweety," my shivering wife will hiss through clenched teeth, her breath visible in the chill air of our kitchen, "Wake up and smell the ice cubes."

The vapor will quickly turn to ice crystals that crash to the floor between us with tiny tinkling sounds. We will stand mesmerized until one of us realizes it's time to thaw out our morning coffee.

"Oh, look dear," she will say, "the cats are trying to climb into

101

the refrigerator to warm up."

Since there is no room to join them among our shelves of moldy science projects, I will head for the shed and our roll of storm windows. That's right, roll -- as in roll of clear plastic sheeting. During the winter months our house often has three sheets to the wind.

Don't get me wrong, we have a sturdy little house, and it's air-tight, except for where the migratory holes are. These holes enjoy our house and want the great outdoors to enjoy it too. In the summer they are down low to afford the local ant communes easy access. In the winter they (the holes) move to higher ground for maximum drip and water stain potential. They are devious, and all on the inaccessible, windswept, rocky, rugged, craggy, steep, treacherous, downhill precipice side of the house where I store my wobbly 52-foot extension ladder.

Well, I don't exactly "store" it there. I have a long tradition of abandoning it there as soon as the last storm sheet is in place. Once I am safely back on the ground and my knees have stopped shaking, I run screaming from the scene.

I do not enjoy heights. Needless to say, this side of the house will not be painted again during my lifetime. Not by me.

Once the plastic is properly in place, our home is truly air-tight. I know this, because if I fire up Chihuahua, our Mexican airless woodstove, we will be close to asphyxiation within 15 minutes. Usually one of the migratory holes senses this and moves to a new location in time to let in enough air to save us.

Sartorially, we become a symphony in natty and nappy flannel, and not just at nap time. In addition to flannel sheets, nightgowns and nightshirts, we own shirts and underwear made of it, and pants, jackets and caps lined with it. In the cold months there are flannel drapes, flannel comforters and pillows strewn around the house, and we used (once) flannel napkins at dinner.

Flannel, in my opinion, just isn't flannel, unless it is plaid. During cool weather, I am the original "Man in the Plaid Flannel Suit." We are proud of the great pains we took to make sure that none of the plaids in the house match each other. On a

typical winter's day there are more loudly-clashing tartans here at Clear Creek Ranch than during the entire history of Scotland.

I'd love to tell you more about wintertime here, but I see the sun is out and I have to go help my wife chip yesterday's frozen laundry off the clothesline.

The Hunt in Gray November

I was admiring the fall color (gray) covering the rocky hillside when my reverie was broken by one of the neighborhood boys walking up the road toward Clear Creek Ranch. I checked for my wallet. This kid only has time for me when there is the possibility that money will change hands -- from mine to his, usually for some fundraising scheme at his school. I don't know what the lifetime limit is, but I'm sure I've reached it as far as losing raffle tickets and over-priced candy bars go.

To be fair, sometimes the kid does offer a tangible service, like lawn mowing, weeding, or firewood stacking. I steeled myself against a leaf-raking proposal. At this time of year I have ten acres covered with uncomposted forest fall-out.

Prepared though I was, he caught me off guard when he asked if I wanted anything shot, trapped, skinned and/or gutted. This young itinerant hitman came equipped for most popular forms of mayhem.

The duffel bag slung over his shoulder contained the family arsenal, and then some. He methodically laid each implement of destruction on the porch as he made his pitch: shotgun, rifle, pistol, knife, sword, harpoon, snare, crossbow, slingshot, spear, axe, blowgun, fly-swatter, frog-gig, garrote wire, leghold trap.

Surely, he insisted, there was a pesky varmint or critter that required immediate splattering, gutting, or bludgeoning somewhere on the property.

Other than the ubiquitous termites, or maybe that ornery old pickup truck of mine, I couldn't think of anything that truly deserved to be put out of its misery. But opening fire on a rusting hunk of metal didn't seem "sporting" to the boy, so he soon packed up and was on his way.

Sporting, sport . . . a physical activity engaged in for pleasure. A lot of sports are adversarial -- evenly matched opponents testing their skill in a game with mutually agreed upon rules. Some consider hunting to be a sport. The only enjoyable part for me would be the stumbling-around-in-the-woods part. Ambushing some animal that's merely minding its own business seems no more "sporting" than a sniper in the school yard.

And yet, it's quite an industry, this hunting-sniping-ambushing thing. Theoretically, after a once-in-a-lifetime purchase of a rifle and/or shotgun, a skilled hunter can supply all his family's protein needs for the cost of a few bullets a year. Of course, as you vegetarian food-gatherers know, the rogue tofu, even during the height of the mating season, is easily (and more economically) subdued with one's bare hands.

In addition to possessing superior fire power and an arsenal of trick lures, deer hunters must "look" the part. Military-style camouflage outerwear, innerwear, underwear, and footwear seems mandatory.

If you aren't armed to the teeth and dressed like a commando or SWAT team member, how can you hope to subdue a shy 80 pound herbivore whose crafty thought processes are pretty much limited to "I hope the buck stops here!", "I'm really in the doe now!" or "What's for lunch?"?

Equally brave are those on midwestern prairie dog safaris, where "hunters" rest their expensive 14 pound scoped rifles on special shooting tables and casually decimate entire coteries and towns of these little creatures for no other reason than target practice.

But I'll reserve my sharpest criticism for the "sport" of Hawaiian-style wild pig stabbing. In that tropical paradise, a guide and his dogs run down wild boars, holding them while his tourist customers stroll up and slash them to death with knives. Perhaps if more folks had to bring home the bacon that way, less of it would be consumed.

Sorry folks, I'm from the outdoorsman school that takes only photos and leaves only footprints. I take shots at animals but they are all of the snap variety. Just turn me loose in the forest armed with an old box Brownie (once I can track it down), and see what develops.

Probably a lot of double-exposed photos with the blur of my thumb in the foreground, as my wife and our photo album will certainly attest.

Half-Baked Thanksgiving

Here at Clear Creek Ranch we are realists. While we grow our own vegetables and bake our own bread, there are some things we know from experience we are just not destined to do. Like bake an edible pumpkin pie. This small flaw can be overlooked 51 weeks of the year, but come late November, I start scouting the town bakeries and other spots where pastry sightings have been reported. I really should go shopping more often . . . or maybe less.

I successfully dodged the dozen towering teenaged skateboarders who apparently are required to live as vagrants on the sidewalks near all supermarkets, where they practice 360°s until they lose consciousness and their skateboards careen wildly into the unsuspecting anklebones of innocent bystanders.

I quadruple-bypassed, without surgery or insurance, the gauntlet of obscenely overweight sample-servers, each clad incongruously in running shoes and jogging outfits, and who offered me skewered tidbits of dietetic cheese-food, meat-food, fruit-food, and cola-food.

I chided myself for thinking of all the laws I'd like to pass to make my visits to town more enjoyable and aesthetically pleasing. Laws that don't exist, but maybe should? Can etiquette or good taste be legislated?

For example: Should all men, regardless of stomach size, be required to wear their belt horizontal to the ground and finally admit they don't still have the 30-inch waist they once had in high school? Should skin-tight jeans be banned on most women over age 18 who weigh more than 120 pounds? Should all restaurant diners have their 49er baseball caps lopped from their heads by roving bands of machete-wielding hat police? Ah, perhaps I expect too much of people.

I found my pumpkin pie neatly sealed in plastic and held in a disposable tinfoil pan (just like the Pilgrims!) and headed for the checkout counter. Against my better judgment I chose the shortest line.

The only customer ahead of me was a grizzled cowboy with a belt buckle the size of a hubcap. His shopping cart was filled with beef jerky strips and cigarettes. The clerk was a trainee and having trouble with the bar code scanner. While I waited patiently, the cowboy repeatedly whistled an absentminded, tunelessly annoying few bars of whatever notes he remembered of Johnny Cash's old hit "Folsom Prison Blues."

Meanwhile behind me at knee-level, I heard what sounded like silverware being dropped down the garbage disposal. I looked down to see a small sniffling urchin loudly inhaling his own mucus while his mother changed his baby sister's diaper in the shopping cart. She scolded the boy in high-decibel babytalk and handed the soiled diaper to the novice clerk, who ran it over the scanner. Then, using the same hand, she fished a tissue from somewhere and held it to the young boy's nose. He obligingly repeated his incredible noise while disgorging several gallons of vile slime into her hand. She handed that to the clerk too. I made a mental note when my turn came to run the pie over the scanner myself.

The whistling cowboy wanted to pay for his purchase using a combination of out-of-state checks, postage stamps, pesos, and what he claimed was the dried ear of a bull. While the clerk got the manager's approval on this bit of international finance, the cowboy continued his tune, consistently missing the same notes, over and over. My pupils dilated and my pulse began to race.

"I shot a man in Safeway just to watch him die," I sang in perfect time to the cowboy's music. "When all I really wanted was to buy a pumpkin pie."

While others stared, the little coughing mucus machine was unimpressed. "I gotta go potty now," he announced to everyone.

I realized I did too. But I was able to hold it (and my pie) until I got back to Clear Creek Ranch. And for that I'm very thankful.

Leftovers From Clear Creek Kitchen

Having more time than money out here at Clear Creek Ranch I have become something of a gourmet chef. For those of you unfamiliar with the term "gourmet," it is pronounced with the "T" missing: gor-may, not gor-met. Gor-met sounds like grommet: those little metal hole reinforcers in old tarps.

Of course, some of my early attempts at haute cuisine should have been pronounced D.O.A. while still in the oven and had said tarp drawn up over them during a moment of silence before being interred directly into the garden compost bin.

During the holiday season many extended families get together to share a special meal. These once festive meals, often harkening back to some common religious, ethnic, or national heritage are ossified into ritualized proceedings. Every year the same family members sit in the same seats around the same dining table groaning under the weight of the same old entrees.

The Buckingham Palace guards seem loose-jointed and lackadaisical when compared to the stifling discipline doled out in the average holiday kitchen. And woe (or whoa) to he or she who tries to spice things up with something new!

Take it from someone who has tried. Everyone in my clan may hate Aunt Erma's cranberry-cabbage casserole, but they'd rather gag down that ghastly gastronomic gunk than run the risk of trying something new.

But you, dear readers are another matter altogether. You are brave and resilient, and most importantly belong to other families than mine. Here, for your holiday dining delight -- two new recipes from the Clear Creek Kitchen.

OLD JACK SOUP

1 head	Garlic, chopped fine
1	Onion, sliced
1 cup	Mushrooms, halved
2 Tbls	Cooking Oil
4 cups	Soup Stock
1 cup	Pumpkin Puree
1 cup	Cream, or Sour Cream
Some	Water, maybe.
Some	Paprika and Parsley

Remove candle wax and/or old light bulb from last month's organic (as opposed to plastic or ceramic) jack-o-lantern which is probably *still* sitting out on the porch if I know you. Cut pumpkin into quarters and bake about an hour at 325° until tender. Scrape out the pulp, apply burn ointment to fingers if you didn't wait for it to cool a bit, then mash the pumpkin all up with your remaining good hand, or run it through an electric blender if you dare. Have one of the kids show you how to plug it in.

In a large pan, saute onions, garlic, and mushrooms lightly in oil. Add soup stock [this can be vegetarian you know], pumpkin puree (above), and salt (if you don't give a tinker's dam about your blood pressure). Simmer for about 30 minutes.

Right before you dish it up, stir in the cream, but don't let it boil! Garnish with parsley, paprika, or anything else that seems appropriate. Note: If your garnish-of-choice includes any old Halloween candies, remove any non-soluble wrappers first.

PUNKIN BUTTER

4 cups	Pumpkin Puree (see above)
1 Tbls	Cinnamon
1 cup	Honey, or other sweetener
¼ Tsp	Ginger
½ Tsp	Cloves, ground (as in "up," not as in "off the")
1	Lemon, the juice of

Toss everything in a heavy saucepan and cook slowly, stirring often, for about an hour. You'll wisely spend this semi-idle time reading up on the horrors of botulism and the proper use of canning jars, if you have any sense at all.

Pour this molten, boiling "butter" into (already) hot, sterilized canning jars and seal them up the way the canning book said to. Small amounts will keep for a while in the refrigerator, but toss it out when the surface starts to look like "after" in one of those late night toupee infomercials.

Until it does, it is superb on toast, muffins, or anything else you'd care to butter up.

Like that rich old relative -- the one with no direct descendants -- who always sits near you at the family feast.

Greetings of the Season

The computer age has insinuated its existence upon us, even in the remote rural reaches where Clear Creek Ranch lies nestled among the pines, and electricity is intermittent at best.

This is the time of year when I take database in hand and purge those ingrates who haven't sent me a card in a few years, and merge the rest of the telephone book onto those little white bulk mail labels.

Does a bulk mailed Christmas greeting seem "cold" to you? Consider the alternative:

In Decembers-past and continuing well into the new year, I was traditionally known as "the claw" around our house -- my hands, temporarily deformed after long bouts of Christmas card envelope addressing.

My wife conveniently blamed her seasonal weight gain (she insists that I mention it is only a pound or two) on all the high-calory paste she ingests while licking stamps and envelope flaps. (I think the brownies she used to "cleanse her palate" after every ten cards may have been a contributing factor, but all that is behind us now.)

No licking -- just sticking. A self-adhesive label on an envelope-less postcard. And so personal, too. Even though the labels are computer generated, I assure you that we personally keyed in each typo-riddled name and address by hand.

Besides, the main thing is the picture or design on the front of the card. We have a unique one. That's what everybody sees when they festoon the room with them this time of year.

Over the years we have progressed through most of the major greeting card styles: serious religious (nativity scenes, guys on camels, a bright elongated star as seen by someone with acute astigmatism), not-so-religious (Blue foiled wishes like: Happy Holidays or Season's Greetings so as not to "offend" our non-Christian friends).

Does anyone actually say "Season's Greetings!" out loud? The only seasonal greetings I associate with December have to do with the weather: "Think it'll ever snow/quit snowing?", "Say is that frostbite?" and "Which travel agent has the best package deal to Tahiti?"

We've also done the forced-smile-family-photo card, where at least one of us is guaranteed to be unhappy with how we look. As well as the cute cartoony anthropomorphic animals (rodents usually) snug in their cozy winter homes. What this has to do with Christmas, I'm not sure. Although in all probability there were rodents somewhere in the manger that first Noel.

And, yes, we are even guilty of penning chatty, self-congratulatory, laden-with-obscure-references family newsletters. Those reams of drivel sure wad up into nice kindling, don't they?

This year's message from Clear Creek Ranch is a simple one. No mention of having a gay old time (don't want to refer to, or offend anyone existing in a sexual subculture), and certainly no paraphrasing classic songs like "may all your Christmases be white" (don't want any racial references or preferences to be misconstrued).

Our message is simplicity itself. A basic greeting. That's it. Hello seemed too formal, and Yo! seemed inappropriate. So here it is: "Hi."

That is the message to all our friends from us here at Clear Creek Ranch this year.

Oh, and if you're reading this in my book paper, don't wait for the card. Please consider yourself seasonally greeted.

I Hereby Resolve?

Most folks pick the first part of the year to make resolutions, short-lived pacts with themselves about self-improvement, usually revolving around dietary discipline or exercise regimens requiring perspiration. Frankly, I don't know where they find the time.

In January my writing hand is still too cramped from all those Christmas cards I signed and thank you notes I wrote in December to be of any use at all. Besides, the memories of yuletide gastronomic excesses and other failures in moderation are still too fresh in my mind for me to attempt any serious improvement.

February is about the time all the January resolutions are broken. "Well, I lasted a month," people say, as if that were quite an achievement. It seems hardly sporting for me to try to duplicate their feat during the shortest month of the year.

I am sorry, SIR! I respectfully refuse to make resolutions in any month whose name sounds like a military command, SIR. Yes SIR! I concede that March owes its name to the mythological god of war, and that dieting can be war, but, SIR, I will burn my meal ticket before I knuckle under to any new attempts at discipline this month.

April? Come on! Lent is over, the Easter Bunny is about to visit . . . and we have a weakness for chocolate bunnies here at Clear Creek Ranch.

Springtime is in full bloom in May. A time of rebirth. A time to smell the roses, and the coffee . . . and shouldn't we stop by that new bakery in town and sample one of each? We need our strength to dance around the May Pole.

For sixteen of my summers, school let out in June. That month has always signified freedom, cutting loose, a time to unwind. Hardly a time to begin disciplining myself.

Independence Day falls in July -- beer and hot dogs (tofu pups now). Four days into the month and I'd be off my diet. It is also the month for vacations, travel, schedule disruptions, fast food on the run, and quaint gourmet restaurants that really depend on our tourist business to survive.

August is county fair month where I live, and I attend all five days. I need that much time to work my way through all the service club-sponsored food booths. I'm very public spirited.

School starts in September -- new school clothes, new teachers, new pencils (update that to floppy disks or whatever kids get now). This would seem to be the ideal month to make resolutions and start anew. But I must be a contrarian, I really hate to be one of the crowd.

And what use is it to start a diet in October? It's the only month of the year guaranteed to end with heaps of candy and sweets all over the house.

November is even worse. There is a traditional government-sponsored gastronomic booby-trap programmed into the fourth Thursday of this month. And then there is the added stress of last minute Christmas shopping.

Obviously December is too late in the year to begin a personal reform movement. Santa needs a longer pattern of good behavior than the three and one-half weeks I have until Christmas. Besides, there is that office party we have to go to. And it wouldn't be polite <u>not</u> to eat, especially after all the trouble someone went to.

Maybe next year . . .

Snapshots

About half the family photo albums here at Clear Creek Ranch are devoted exclusively to snapshots of our two cats. These cats are not show cats, they are no exotic breed. Plain old Tuxedo cats, one black-and-white, the other grey-and-white. Not just house cats, our family.

As far as I know they don't keep photos of us, but that doesn't stop my wife and me from snapping away at the least provocation. The smallest hint of cuteness is apt to set us (and the flash bulbs) off. One roll a month, an average 36 exposures, twelve months a year, for over fifteen years.

To be honest, we must have hundreds of variations on the same poses although it isn't immediately evident because the photos are filled chronologically. Thus the fifteen shots of them nestled cutely among the presents under fifteen different Christmas trees have some breathing room between them. Hundreds of them sprawled on their backs luxuriating in most unladylike poses beneath the toasty warmth of the woodstove. Or sprawled on their backs inelegantly on the windowsill catching a cool summer breeze.

The camera doesn't inhibit them. Nothing much does. If a photo session lasts too long, they simply walk away, tail held high, the tip flicking, giving the cameraman a rear view reminiscent of tiny fur covered jodhpurs.

Nothing about their bodies seems to embarrass them. Or anything about mine for that matter. They've seen me both clothed and naked in tonnages that fluctuate from "fighting trim" to "beached whale," groggy with morning breath and Albert Einstein's hairdo, or slicked down and spiffed up, dressed to the nines (whatever the nines may be). The cats don't care about any of that, except perhaps the nines part, and then only if it has to do with their fabled nine lives.

They are a comfort when I'm sad or troubled. Cynics would say they are only after a warm lap to sit on, but I know better. For starters my lap is rather skimpy, a precarious perch, but one they seek out regularly. They've even come to tolerate the smell of the "other" cat in my life.

It's not like I'm cheating on them or anything. But the Pet

Adoption Thrift Store where I volunteer my time has a store cat and over time we've attached ourselves to each other. Every cat has a different temperament and personality (purr-sonality, my wife likes to say).

The first few times I came home after Fiona (the store cat) rubbed against my pants leg, our house cats were intrigued by the new smell. I felt like a cheating husband who walks into the house with lipstick on his collar -- she (the other cat) was that obvious to their discerning noses.

Fiona probably smelled the house cats on me, but she never let on. She was a stray, a street cat. Glad to have a warm dry place to sleep, plenty of food, and people who loved her. My wife and I often talked about taking her home. We could adjust to more cats on the bed with us, I thought. If the cats could adjust to each other, that is.

Well, it never happened.

Fiona was with us for almost two years, greeting me when I opened up the store, demanding breakfast, supervising my every move. A very vocal cat. She spent her days sitting stubbornly on top of the jewelry display case and blocking everything from the customers view until she got enough strokes. Then maybe, just maybe, she'd move. Usually to a spot where she could drape her tail over a customer's hand as he tried to write a check.

In mid-December she began to lose weight. Her breathing was labored. We had always known that Fiona had leukemia, an unpredictable disease. According to the veterinarians, she might live a normal life span, and then again she might not. Each case is different and there is no known cure.

Two days before Christmas we had to make a decision, a hard one for me. Fiona was in a lot of pain by then and was never going to get any better. She had to be euthanized. I'd make a Doctor Cat-vorkian joke here, except there was nothing funny about it.

My wife and I were with Fiona when she got the injection. For a moment she got up as if she was going to run. Then she settled down, her chin on her paws. And in a few seconds she was gone.

But not forgotten. She was part of my family.

Rough Growing On The Roof

When we designed guest accommodations here at Clear Creek Ranch, one of our major concerns was disturbing the land -- we didn't want to. "Low impact" was the operative word.

I suggested spartan guest quarters consisting of a sleeping bag under the stars with some seasonal, and politically-correct, adjustments: a can of insect repellant (non-aerosol) in springtime, and perhaps a tarp (vegetable fiber-based) to keep the sleet at bay in the dead of winter.

While my wife agreed that such an arrangement would have little or no impact on the environment or our anorectic checkbook balance, she felt it would have a negative impact on our houseguests, unless we happened to be hosting a team of Alaskan sled dogs just back from a trek to the Pole.

I sensed immediately that this low-impact guest house idea was destined to have a considerably larger impact on the lower reaches of my aged back and the diminishing resources of my withered brain than I had originally reckoned.

Underground housing was one option that wouldn't spoil the view. And if it doesn't work out, I thought, I can just bury my mistake.

"A hole in the ground," my wife sniffed dismissively.

"Earth-sheltered living space," I countered.

"I can dig it . . . if you dig it," she eventually smiled.

My wife's vocalizations aren't hopelessly stuck in 25-year-old slang speech patterns. Her comment was simply a gentle reminder of my last excavation attempt -- the one that resulted in the mossy combination wine-cellar-frog-pond beneath our house. Anyone care for a seep of homemade wine from a moss-covered bottle?

So rather than risk hitting another hidden spring and singing the subterranean home-slick blues again, we compromised on the design, but not on our principles. We hired a backhoe from a professional digger named Doug (I'm sorry, but that's his name) and notched a tiny building pad site in the hillside overlooking the pond.

The construction was traditional, with some allowances engineered in for the extra load on the roof. Instead of the usual shingles, tiles, or tin, we went with sod -- a dirt roof, two feet deep in places.

Of course a good deal of that "ran off" after the first heavy rain. It didn't run far, forming random mounds of silt around the little structure. I tried to call them "decorative berms" and lobbied to plant them with wildflowers. But my wife rejected my last ditch effort at a shovel-free existence. It took two long days to get all the dirt back up where it belonged. I coined the new verb "re-sodomize," and my wife immediately un-coined it.

Erosion control became prominent in my thoughts as I lay maladjusted on the chiropractor's table. But I also thought of functionality. Our rock-infested clay soil made digging difficult. Septic system leach lines needed to be installed somewhere to service our bucolic bungalow. The roof of which was covered with about 900 cubic feet of unobstructed permeable soil. It was perfect.

"Let me see if I understand all the nuances of this complex engineering concept," my wife said sweetly. "You are proposing to install on the roof, intentionally, pipes that are designed to leak."

We planted grass seed instead.

It thrived, and our little cottage soon had a full head of green hair, which needed regular trimming. This could have been easily accomplished with the lawnmower, if the roof had been flat. It was tedious work pushing the mower back and forth, with my uphill leg flexed and my downhill leg overextended. I began wearing a built-up shoe on my downhill foot, which I had

to constantly switch back and forth as I changed directions. A ten minute job now took all morning.

The next year we took out the lawn and planted a vegetable garden there. It seems to be working out okay, except for some of the longer varieties of carrot, which dangle in the air inside the ceiling like hairy orange stalactites.

And when my wife suggested we expand the cottage some time in the future, I immediately planted a series of douglas fir tree seedlings around the perimeter of the roof so the studs for our second floor walls can grow in place.

Eventually that will be another story.

Thrushes, Thrips, and Thistles

One of the first books I bought after moving to the country was the classic "A Field Guide to Western Birds" written and illustrated by the late Roger Tory Peterson.

The reason was simple. Every day over my morning coffee, I'd see dozens of different types of birds outside my window. As a city boy, I only recognized the three major types of outdoor city birds: pigeons, seagulls, and the fugitive parakeet.

As a birdwatching neighbor pointed out, my "life list" was woefully incomplete. Mr. Peterson's book contains, among many fine color illustrations and silhouettes, a checklist of all the known bird varieties frequenting the Western US, although not necessarily the orchard outside my kitchen window.

To make significant headway on my list, I'd have to go thrashing around in the muck and mosquitoes of wetland wildlife refuges. Which I did a few times, startling birds and binoculared birdwatchers in equal numbers. (Is there a life list available for birdwatcher-types?). And my picky neighbor insisted it was cheating to check off birds I'd seen caged in zoos or stuffed in museums. According to him, claiming a sighting of a rare specimen on a PBS-TV wildlife special was simply out of the question.

I soon crossed him off my "neighbor life list" (the grossbeaked belly-acher) and decided formal birdwatching was out -- too many rules and too much roadwork. I cast about for an outdoor hobby that could be done sitting down on the screen porch. I needed to look no farther than my garden.

Over the years I've tried to improve the soil in our garden. But the part that isn't granite boulders insists on reverting quickly to adobe bricks regardless of the amounts of organic matter I import from nearby ranches and heap there annually.

I've tried all the available manures: steer, horse, chicken, pig, sheep, rabbit, llama, and ostrich, to name a few. The only thing I've achieved is to introduce new varieties of undigested weed seeds with each new batch of manure. The weed seeds, of course, have no trouble thriving within my garden walls and choking the life from anything I might intentionally plant there.

Thank goodness for "Weeds of California," a 500 page, illustrated Department of Agriculture publication I stumbled upon in a Thrift Shop book department. Until I read it, weeds had no variety to me -- they were just the predominant green life force in the garden.

"The weeds are out of control," my wife would say.

"Ground cover," I'd correct. "They keep the dust down."

"The shade trees we planted back in '84 are dying because the groundcover is blocking their sun."

About then in the conversation I'd go out to the garden with a chainsaw and thin the groundcover down to manageable levels -- nothing higher than six or seven feet.

But now, I'm working on my "life list" of weeds. It would be madness to "weed" the garden. My weed bible includes their latin names, which I use whenever my neighbor the bird expert goes weed-watching with me.

There are over 10,000 species of the thistle family alone. Thistles include such edible varieties as artichokes and lettuce, ornamentals like chrysanthemums, dahlias, and marigolds, as well as 9,995 types of thistle weeds, many hundreds of which are presently flourishing in my garden.

And there are so many other species and varieties: milkweed, nettles, figwort, witchgrass, pokeweed, tansy -- the list is almost endless. I'm constantly sighting new ones in my botanical petting zoo, often from the comfort of my screen porch, thanks to the high-powered binoculars I acquired back during my birdwatching period.

The diversity in the garden has even attracted other admirers, most of whom are vegetarian -- insects. Garden pests? Once maybe, but not now. You see I just unearthed another volume, entitled "The Gardener's Bug Book."

Now I'm bug-watching too. Another list to complete. What started out as an hobby has almost become a full time job. If this keeps up, I might be forced to go back to ordinary gardening just to get some rest.

Have A Berry Nice Day

Nature can be very wasteful. Take blackberries for example. We've got about an acre of them growing in a thick tangle downhill from our spring here at Clear Creek Ranch. In season they produce thousands, perhaps millions of juicy, sweet, blue-black berry clusters.

When we first purchased our property we didn't know what to do with such a bonanza, but the local wildlife did. The deer browsed as high as they could reach on the outer edges of the patch. When those canes were bare, they moved on to easier pickings -- in our rose garden.

The sweetest berries, of course, were in the impenetrable interior of the patch, where each cluster was protected by a phalanx of bloodthirsty thorns. Having torn myself to shreds in a futile quest after these succulent beauties, I forfeited all future rights to the airborne division: the neighborhood birds.

The ease with which they feasted upon their bounty irked me. Some perched on the very thorns that still bore traces of my shirt threads and dried blood. And the feathered freeloaders were so reckless and wasteful. A single peck at each berry cluster and then on to the next. Most of the fruit rotted where it hung. Things had to change.

That autumn I rented a brush clearing machine and mowed a maze-like series of intersecting rows through the patch so I'd have access to the next summer's crop. To thwart the deer, who would have treated these new rows like additional aisles at the open air grocery store, I mowed a single entrance to the maze and secured it with an eight foot high wire gate.

This system worked great, as long as I remembered to close the gate. Soon we were feasting on bucketsful of the luscious berries. But even a steady diet of caviar and champagne gets old, I am told. (No one's ever given me a first hand opportunity to research this, but I will consider any offers in this direction.)

Our berry-lust was sated long before the bushes quit producing, so we hunted for new outlets for our harvest. Unfortunately, the few neighbors who would admit to eating anything that didn't start out with hooves, fur, and/or feathers were already inundated with their own berry crops.

"How about a roadside stand," my wife suggested.

I told her of my bitter disappointment as a youthful lemonade entrepreneur on a lightly-traveled cul-de-sac somewhere deep within a bland tract development in outer-suburbia. My only sale had been to the neighborhood mailman. And even those sales figures were artificially inflated. (Mom, if you're reading, I've never mentioned this, but I saw you hand him that dime when he dropped off our mail just before he stopped at my stand).

Still, we had bushels of berries rotting on our screen porch and one of our neighbors had an abandoned vegetable stand out by the county road. It was a ramshackle affair, with sagging roof and peeling paint and had belonged to someone named Chuck, because "Chuck's" was scrawled in large free-hand letters on both sides. According to my neighbor, weekend traffic on the road was brisk, and chockful of rich foreigners from the city.

That weekend I carted my berries to the stand, hand painted my own addendum to Chuck's magnificent work: "berry's." I know that's the wrong spelling. But a dyslexic haze shrouded my brain as soon as I picked up the paintbrush. In addition to the Y' where the IE should have been, the first R was flipped backwards so its little leg pointed to the left. I adjusted my overalls, settled down with my crossword puzzle and nibbled on berries while I waited for my public to discover me.

Several hours later, when most of the berries were gone, they did. By then my hands, lips, and shirtfront were stained blue with berry juice. A carload of little kids stared at me like I was the tattooed carnival man. Their mother asked if I had restroom facilities for her squirming urchins. I pointed a blue finger toward the bushes behind the shed, and even offered my crossword puzzle if she was in need of paper products.

"Give me a map back to civilization, you blue-faced yahoo!" she screeched. I extracted a waterlogged map from my truck glove box and she flipped me a $10 bill, not waiting for change.

Slight variations on this scenario repeated themselves throughout the day. A little "idea light" twinkled in my brain.

The roadside stand is now fruitless, but fruitful, despite an irate visit from the Apostrophe Abuse Council. Chuck's Berry's now houses a road map vending machine and two pay toilets. Business is brisk, and I don't even have to be there.

The outhouse, of course, is known as the Johnny B Goode.

Cereal Killer

"I want your hot buns," I said crossly.

"Let's see your dough, you loafer," came the reply.

But I had no dough, nor did my wife. We wanted bread but the pantry was bare. The Clear Creek Ranch bunkhouse was understaffed with the "staff of life." No amount of flour-y speech could leaven the seriousness of that fact. In short, our flour sack was empty.

"I have a germ of an idea," my wife said. "Why don't we grow our own flour plants?"

"Well, for starters, beloved fellow green-thumb," I chaffed, "I would expend much less energy if I walked back and forth into town (20 miles each way) and toted home several hundred pounds of the stuff on my back."

"Relax, my suburban plowboy. No need for gruel and unusual measures. It says right here in Grain, Grain, Grow Away that a 20'x50' plot is sufficient for a family our size."

"Ah," I said ryely.

I couldn't believe it. Even my dusty reference library, always a reliable source of procrastination strategies, was turning its cracked spines against me.

I was soon sowing my wild oats (well, red wheat actually) in the freshly-tilled soil. But my wheatfield was no flat square of green like the miles of prairie cornfields that stretched to the horizon in the movie "Field of Dreams." There was more level land in the baseball diamond batter's box in that movie than there is in all of Clear Creek Ranch.

I took a wheaten-sea attitude, but we did, in fact, soon had amber waves of grain. Since the wheatfield was sown in undulating soil it had a wavy appearance even on breezeless days. Some of my seed fell on the ever-present boulders (diminutive purple mountains majesty) and unfortunately

125

withered and died. But enough sprouted so that I was faced with the grim prospect of reaping.

More conflict. I wanted to cut everything down with my weedwhacker (the mechanical solution), but my wife reminded me about all the pollutants in the gasoline fumes. We opted for the organical solution. Unfortunately, the only manual cutting device we owned was a pair of shears better suited for clipping the odd rosebud.

I set to work and in less than an hour I had harvested enough wheat for a fair-sized muffin. It was time for a break. I sought the shade of the nearest boulder and gazed into space. It was a warm, drowsy day. Overhead a redtailed hawk effortlessly spiralled upward riding the unseen thermal currents.

"Here's a scythe for soar eyes," my wife said, handing me the lethal looking implement.

"Where is yours?" I asked.

"Laugh and the world laughs with you," came her answer. "Reap, and you reap alone."

But she did bring me lunch in the field. It was an assortment of grain-related products: wheatgrass tea, and both porridge and gruel (there's a fine distinction). She set it in the field ahead of me as a surprise. It was. When I found it the tea and the gruel had mixed together and everything was covered with cut grain.

"I love to wheat my eaties," I said.

It wasn't long before the flailing and winnowing started. That was how I separated the wheat from the rest of the stuff. As an upper body workout, you can't beat flailing and winnowing.

It was a hot day, the sun blazed overhead. All my huffing and puffing attracted our cats' attention. They sat in the shade of a nearby boulder and supervised. Soon they and the rocks were covered with winnowed wheat. I noticed that the sun actually roasted the grain on the rocks, but that the grain on the cats was okay (if you don't mind a little cat hair).

"Our politically-correct friends will love your pastries now," I announced to my wife. "Our wheat is un-toasted on animals."

"And gruel/tea free."

Uncorking a Fine Whine

In the morning I planted two little grape vines between massive wooden support posts. In the afternoon I broke ground on the wine cellar. That's the kind of guy I am, optimistic, farsighted -- in short, a dreamer.

By the time the first leaves sprouted on those tiny grape-bearing twigs, I had broken a little more ground on the cellar, but not much. I had, however, taken delivery on enough pallets of used brick to line the walls of the un-dug cellar, a massive chandelier to light its shadowy confines, and an industrial strength sump pump.

This last item became necessary when I found myself standing in several inches of water as I swung my pick. Wine cellars are supposed to be cool and maybe damp. But even novice vintners such as I know that the fancy labels won't stick to the bottles if the waters start to rise. And when I am busy knocking back an estate bottled aperitif with visiting royalty or friends, I don't want to be confused as to which of my two vines has contributed the squeezings.

The puny vines bore no fruit that first year. And while it looked like they might the next year, all I got was a handful of tiny raisins when the drip irrigation system clogged during a crucial month. Meanwhile the water was flowing freely in my still partially-excavated wine cellar.

"Wine grotto is more like it," my wife said.

The pallets of used bricks were beginning to develop an interesting mossy patina from their multi-year-round exposure to the damp. I hung the oversized chandelier "temporarily" from the garage ceiling and found that I couldn't park my car under it. My unsheltered car began to develop a rusty patina of its own.

Which was a small price to pay. I needed the garage floor space for the winemaking paraphernalia which was quickly accumulating there. It was quite a collection: wine press, strainers, fermentation vats, five gallon jugs, valves, test tubes, funnels, corking tools, floggers, casks, hydrometers and litmus papers.

I felt inadequate among these exacting devices and enrolled at a mail order university. Like the exotic yeasts necessary for winemaking, I knew I could rise to the challenge. By working diligently most week-nights, I figure I should earn the requisite Master's Degree in Chemistry some time after the turn of the century. We may celebrate the occasion with a bottle of my homegrown wine. If my calculations are correct that will be the first year we may have enough grapes to endure a proper stomping.

Meanwhile I acquired some British winemaking manuals which offered recipes for "wine" made from almost any fermentable non-meat food product that may be purchased in a can. This includes all the predictable canned fruits, as well as snapbeans, marrow (zucchini) and parsnips, to name a few. Canned fruit is recommended because it usually contains sugar, which the yeast cells (living organisms) digest and turn into alcohol. To put it another way, that glow you get after a few swallows of wine was caused by yeast droppings. Cheers!

My wife and I tried our hand (make that feet) at banana wine. I bought a few cases of over-ripe bananas and spent two days coaxing her into the stomping vat. Since she usually has the cleaner feet, and often says so, I knew she wouldn't drink anything I'd stomped. Her facial expressions were priceless as she gooshed around in there. Well, maybe not priceless, I am getting $100 each for the Polaroids I had the presence of mind to snap.

After months of fermenting, racking and re-racking, my chemistry set told me the wine was ready. The only problem was that when I held it up to the light, it resembled grapefruit juice - - which is to say it lacked clarity.

"Chateau de Clear Creek Ranch seems like an unfortunate label choice," I said cloudily.

"Uk! What an impertinent bouquet," my wife sniffed. "Chateau de Flip Flop sounds more like it."

I wasn't bold enough to remind her whose feet had been where.

But the fancy labels sure look good in those dark green bottles we bought. We are laying aside several cases in the inflatable raft floating in the wine cellar. They should make wonderful surprise gifts for those "special someones" in our lives.

Until We Mead Again

One of my neighbors left town suddenly owing me a lot of money. He slipped a note in my mailbox saying that I ought to appropriate what I wanted from his barn before the rest of his creditors started swarming about. That took some of the sting out of my financial loss. There wasn't much to choose from, but a stack of shabby-looking beekeeping boxes in the corner caught my eye. They would be good for storage, I thought. Or, if they were too far gone, I could chop them up for kindling. The boxes were heavier than I expected and the lids were on tight, so I loaded the truck and buzzed on home.

My wife was watching as I pried open the first box.

"Any money, honey?" she asked.

"No honey. But there is honey, honey," I said.

"I love honey, honey," she smiled.

We both liked honey, but had no idea what to do with 400 pounds of it. Our other neighbors wouldn't buy it even though it tasted great. The problem was the color, which was an unappetizing shade of grey. What to do?

As usual the answer came as we reflected on the snippets of a PBS documentary during the interminable pledge breaks. The show, entitled "Norse Code," and sponsored (excuse me, underwritten) by the Fjord Foundation, dealt with everyday life among Viking-types a thousand years ago.

"Didn't the vikings drink mead from staghorn flagons?" I asked.

"Uk! That's probably why so few of them are pillaging Europe today."

"One man's mead, is another man's poison," I agreed. But I was excited. "Mead is made from honey. We can make our own honey wine!"

Vivid visions of our last winemaking escapade flashed before

129

my wife's eyes. It had been ripe banana wine.

"Count mead out," she said. "I'm not stomping around in a vat filled with honey combs while you take pictures and giggle."

"You have a fine memory for detail," I said, trying to salvage something from the conversation.

So it was I who donned some old, but clean, argyle socks and hopped up and down on the honey combs until they (and my footwear) began to release their essence. It was like putting my feet in grey Jell-O. In retrospect, the stomping probably wasn't necessary, but I am something of a traditionalist when it comes to winemaking.

A handy hint if you try this: unless you are adept at walking on your hands, decide how you will transport yourself to clean-up facilities <u>before</u> you step into the stomping vat.

I siphoned the murky liquid, along with the yeast and other ingredients into five-gallon winemaking jugs. I told myself that everything would settle to the bottom during the filtration process . . . like the green and red argyle sock fibers (or were those leg hairs?) that swirled about in the gloom. I shared the uncertainty of novice winemakers everywhere. But uncertainty and winemaking are both centuries-old traditions in my family. I began to wax nostalgic for the good old daze, and I certainly had the residual beeswax to do it.

I also looked forward to the day when I could tip back my horned battle helmet and lounge in my castle as I enjoyed a staghorn filled with my own honey wine and a plate of french fries. (I'm a mead and potatoes man, you see). But mostly I envisioned the day when I could present visitors to Clear Creek Ranch with a gallon or two of our estate bottled grey stuff as they headed home.

"Until we mead again," I'd say.

A New Program for Problem Plinkers

Quite a few people who live out in the country near me should face the facts, join A.A., and get into a 12-step program.

Now don't get all huffy, you are probably thinking of that other A.A. The A.A. I am speaking about is Ammunition-users Anonymous. It caters to those folks addicted to the use and abuse of everything from BB guns to assault rifles. On a typical spring Saturday morning near Clear Creek Ranch the hills are alive with the sound of gunfire.

I interviewed one prospective member who preferred to remain anonymous. (I will call him "Bud," taken from the name stenciled on his gimme ball cap). "Bud" had the following to say, more or less. I took the liberty of re-conjugating his verbs and eliminating the many hoots and grunts and other sound effects for coherence's sake.

"Sure I use ammo, a lot of ammo, but only for target practice. Old bottles, cans, that sort of thing. We call it 'plinking.' My daddy taught me, and before that, his daddy taught him. All true Americans plink. I admit that I plink a lot, but I don't have a plinking problem."

Since "Bud" was heavily armed during the interview, I decided not to discuss the possible onomatopoeic origins of the verb "to plink," or to confront him with his flawed syllogisms and his obvious attempts at "denial." I have observed that this is a fairly common behavior pattern among long-time heavy plinkers.

A.A. suggests a disarmingly simple strategy: cold turkey withdrawal. Studies show that "tapering off" just doesn't work. Moving down from an AK-47 to an old Daisy air rifle is progress, experts concede, but experts stress that the move from heavy plinking to light plinking is still plinking. Some members get to the point where they no longer carry anything in their pick-up truck gun racks, but a careful search of their pockets usually turns up a "favorite bullet" that they are keeping in reserve "just in case," or a photo of a favorite weapon torn furtively from the latest issue of Guns and Ammo.

When A.A. members "fall off the wagon," they generally abandon the wagon in a nearby vacant lot and let it rust for a while before filling it full of bullet holes. But a true addict won't stop there. If there are any unspent bullets left after they've recreated the slow motion death scene from "Bonnie & Clyde," they immediately fix their sights on the livestock.

I can't tell you how many times I've come across tiny black cows laying bullet-riddled by the side of the road. The poor little guys -- most of them no more than 12 inches long from nose to tail -- should know better than to stand in profile against the yellow background of those Cattle
X-ing signs. Slow-moving fenceposts, mailboxes, and even abandoned buildings (especially the windows) haven't got a chance when a serious plinker is on a shooting spree.

This senseless wanton slaughter of inanimate objects would stop if A.A. members would live up to the promise they made during their first meeting: to always eat what they shoot. How does cajun-style sound? A mess of blackened cans and bottle shards anyone?

Of course, no one can be helped unless they want to be helped. First and foremost, the problem plinker must acknowledge that he (plinkers are predominantly, although not exclusively, male) has a problem.

If you suspect you might need the program, but aren't sure, look for these telltale signs in your own behavior. When you look at an empty dog food can before you toss it into the trash, does your trigger finger begin to itch? Does the mere smell of gun oil cause your ears to start ringing? Can you rattle off ballistics specifications of every type of ammunition manufactured since WWII, but the middle names and birthdays of your children escape you?

Help is available. Call Ammunition-users Anonymous now and enroll in their voluntary (and some say controversial) nintendo program now.

Something "Wickered" This Way Comes

It was in one closet or another, or in the garage, or on a shelf in the shed for as long as I could remember. It was over fifteen years old, had travelled hundreds of miles to one house after another, and yet it remained brand new, un-used. It was a wedding present. One of those peculiar "occasional" pieces held in reserve for an occasion that had never happened, yet.

One spring morning I sat on the porch admiring the view. The honey bees were busy pollinating the orchardette in our side yard and the apple blossoms provided a brilliant canopy overhead. A gentle breeze jostled the pink and white petals and as they fell they carpeted the thick new grass. What a perfect day for lazing about.

I remembered a time when on days like this the whole family would pile into the car and drive to a park somewhere outside of town. The kids would climb trees or splash about in the stream terrorizing tadpoles while the adults did whatever adults did until it was time to eat. Then we would all gather around the checkered cloth at a splintery table under a big tree and stuff ourselves with all the goodies mom had packed in the basket.

A sturdy wicker picnic basket with a hinged lid. Just like the virginal one we now had out in the shed. I took it down and dusted it off. What a marvel of efficiency it was: compartments filled with silverware, plates, napkins, and glasses. There was a checkered table cloth, wine glasses and an old unopened bottle of champagne. Toss in a little food, and we'd be ready to go.

"Go where?" my wife asked.

"On a picnic," I enthused.

"I'm not budging. This is my day off."

In her own charmingly blunt way she was expressing a certain wisdom. There was, indeed, no need to "go" anywhere. Clear Creek Ranch has its own stream, trees and bushes beyond number, and countless picturesque al fresco eating sites, providing, in some cases, that the diners are not too picky about what picture they gaze upon as they wolf down a second helping of "SomeMores."

But there are beautiful secluded spots, small meadows covered with wildflowers, a seasonally babbling brook, and on one aerie outcropping -- if one stands on tippy-toe -- a panoramic western view of the coastal range some hundred miles distant.

I toyed with the alternatives as I ransacked the refrigerator to compile the ingredients for our feast. Deviled eggs, patriotic potato salad (made from red, white, and blue potatoes), chocolate layer cake, pink lemonade, a thermos of espresso, a jar of homemade dill pickles, and of course the requisite graham crackers, marshmallows and slabs of milk chocolate for building SomeMores. In short, an antacid vendor's dream menu.

We wore white, a color that symbolizes purity, rebirth, renewal . . . and stupendous naivety if one is planning a hike in the woods. As we lifted the loaded basket it creaked and groaned, but not nearly as much as our backs did. And there were hammocks, kites, lawn chairs and frisbees to consider. I quickly hosed off the wheelbarrow we use to transfer compost around the garden, and pressed it into service. Then we wended our way up through groves of pubescent poison oak to the secret spot I'd found.

The champagne cork came out easily, no pop or foam, with a heavy scent of vinegar. Ah, well. We had just unfurled the postage-stamp-sized table cloth when the guests began to arrive. Mosquitos, big billowing clouds of them. Famished. And I'd forgotten the repellant.

"What about all those mosquito-eating fish you stocked in the pond?" my wife asked.

"If they can walk up the hill on their own, they are welcome here," I said, as I headed home for the repellant. A swarm of meat-eating bees hurried past me on the trail. But we had no repellant at home. The best I could do was two khaki-colored hoods covered with netting. It would be tough straining a gooey SomeMore through that.

As I scrambled up the hill I noticed morbidly hopeful buzzards circling overhead. I quickened my pace. My wife was holding her own against the ravenous insects, flailing away with the frisbee and empty champagne bottle, piles of tiny carcasses heaped at her feet. She'd used the bottle's contents on her skin as an experimental repellant. I got a whiff, and it sure worked for me . . . but not against the bug battalions. We beat a hasty retreat home.

The next time I feel like a change of scenery during mealtime, we'll just switch places at the dinner table.

Cross Over Crossed Wires

Last Sunday afternoon the key snapped off in the ignition switch of my old pickup truck. Try as I might, I couldn't get it started. I attempted to extract the broken piece, but only drove it in deeper. Even if I had been successful it wouldn't have done me much good. The only other ignition key I had was ten miles away at home -- safely attached to my wife's key ring. I knew she was out puttering in the Clear Creek Ranch vegetable garden/weedpatch, and not about to answer the telephone.

I assessed my alternatives. Abandonment -- I'd threatened to do that every time something else on that 24 year-old vehicle wore out, rusted through, fell off, or exploded. I was even stranded at the perfect location -- the county dump. I figured I could push it as far as the scrap metal pile.

The only thing that stopped me was the thought of all the lives I'd be disrupting -- family members: brothers, sisters, parents, cousins, batty old great aunts. It wasn't my family I had in mind, but a certain large extended family that has established a colony somewhere under the seat cushions.

Once upon a time I forgot a small open jar of doggie treats on the floor of the truck -- an easy thing to do, as you would know if you've every seen the clutter in the cab of my truck. When I retrieved the container a few days later, it was empty. There were tiny droppings on the dashboard which I attributed at the time to an incontinent mouse. It had plenty of means of entry. In my truck, the floorboards are actually boards and gaping holes abound.

But then I realized that the food had disappeared from an upright, slick-sided glass jar. Unless the mouse had a tiny ladder or was able to rappel down the glassy precipice with mountaineering (mouseneering?) equipment, something else was afoot. Or aflight, actually. The evening sky around our place is thick with bloodthirsty insects and fortunately for us, equally ravenous bats. During daylight hours the bats squeeze into any old crevice or corner to digest things.

While rooting around under the front seat one day I noticed a few of them hanging around on the springs. I might have done something about them, but I was distracted by the large mound of pocket change that had accumulated behind the seat over the years. Nickels, dimes, quarters, halves -- over fifty dollars-worth. I banked the money, the bats stayed.

My truck is idle most of the time, and the windows don't crank up all the way, so it is a perfect (bat) mobile home. We co-exist peacefully, although I do wish they'd do their business somewhere other than on the dashboard. Still, I couldn't leave them so far from home. Abandonment was out.

Try contacting a locksmith on a Sunday afternoon. On the other hand, don't waste your time. You will also have to contact your banker -- to swing the second mortgage required to finance the premium rates the local Lock Guy charges on weekends. His minimum rate would have more than cleaned out that horde of coins I'd recently discovered.

In the movies and on TV, keyless car thieves are always reaching under the dashboard, fiddling with some ignition wires for about two seconds, and then driving down the highway. It's called hot-wiring, and the camera never shows a close-up of what's actually going on. This may be to avoid criticism from groups claiming that such scenes only encourage car theft. But I think the real pressure is coming from the Auto Parts Stores cartel.

It is very easy to connect all those wires and get the engine going. But the movies never told me about the not-so-hot wire -- the one that goes to the starter. That's the one you have to disconnect once the engine is running.

Well you don't have to, I didn't. I was so overjoyed that I was driving away from the deafening sounds of all that heavy equipment at the dump that I didn't notice the new whining noise coming from under the hood. It was the sound of my flywheel chewing all the teeth off the starter. By the time I got home the noise had stopped.

And, of course, the truck wouldn't start again without some significant repairs -- about three skinned knuckles and fifty dollars-worth of auto parts. I'm writing to Siskel and Ebert (and maybe Manny, Moe & Jack) to complain.

Shelf-ish Thoughts

In the town near Clear Creek Ranch, if something is a hundred years old, it is considered ancient. If it is older than that -- say 125 years old -- folks start searching the cellar for cave paintings of mastodons, or dinosaur droppings near the cornerstone.

My favorite local structure is the public library. It was built with a Carnegie grant, quite some time ago. Andrew Carnegie, the famous steelmaker and philanthropist, used much of his wealth to build 2,500 libraries, among other things.

He built the one in my town to last a while. It is a solid, snug two-story building, set on a tree covered lot behind the business district, within easy walking distance for many town residents. It could be a nice spot to visit during a weekly shopping spree in town. Or a storekeeper's quiet refuge during lunch hour. Or a cozy place to duck into during a sudden cloudburst. A place to catch up on the latest from newspapers hung on wooden rods like so many towels.

The bookshelves extend to the 12-foot ceilings and the windows do too. The massive librarian's counter are hardwood, elegant, finely-crafted, ornately carved. The wood is burnished dark from age, and polish, and the many hands that clutched the thousands of books that resided there, between brief sorties to the desks and coffee tables of readers throughout the county.

There was a time when I was a boy, that I'd go to a library like this one, to get a book to read, or to research a paper I was writing for school. I'd open the book up and look at the card in the pocket. I wanted to see who had last checked out the book. All the names were handwritten by the borrowers. I'd rarely know the people, but some times I did. Some times I'd discover I was the first person to check out this particular book in ten or twenty years, but it appeared to have been real popular for a while back then. Somehow it's nice to know the history of the book you're reading.

Of course, there is no more fitting your signature into a tiny space, or paper library cards for that matter. I had one a few years ago that had a little metal plate with my name embossed on it. When I got a book, the librarian put my card into a machine that worked like the ones that handle credit card receipts. The embossed part left a permanent imprint on my wallet.

But it's all computers now. More efficient, I suppose. But a lot less romantic. In a literal sense, I think I know how artificially inseminated cows must feel. It's so impersonal. Did other people like this book enough to check it out? Nobody knows except the computer. And just try getting it to talk to you, even in a library whisper.

Sadly, "progress" has come to my town. I can only guess at the reasons -- the building was too small, had too many steps to be wheelchair accessible, library construction funds from some state or federal program suddenly became available on a use-it-or-lose-it basis. The fact is, the library I describe above was closed as a public library.

A new library, vastly superior (or at the very least, vast) was built on an out-of-the-way hilltop overlooking the county's administration offices on the far side of a major highway that runs through town. Nobody from town "just drops in" on the librarian anymore. They need to get in a car and drive there. I hope they find the doors open more often than I have.

This library is open five days a week, but with different hours on three of the five days. They publish their hours, but I never have the list with me when I need it. The confusion is compounded by another nearby library (still in it's quaint old centrally-located brick building for now) with its own five day schedule of variable hours.

The new library has the dimensions of a cathedral. You could stack a dozen of Carnegie's libraries inside it. But it doesn't have many more books than it did before the move. "The funds" aren't available for stocking it. I guess there is more political hay to be made in construction than in book buying. And now the county is talking about cutting back the hours the libraries will be open. (Probably a prelude to closing down the other old conveniently located one).

Why not close the library system altogether? Using a politician's logic -- since they won't have to buy any books, think of all the trees they can save!

No need for the government to ban or burn books anymore, they just make them inaccessible.

A Cure For Certain Post-Partum Blues

For the first time in fifteen years I did not attend the local county fair. I seem to be the only person in the county who did not attend. Or at least the only person who admits to having no acceptable excuse for non-attendance.

For example, the dog did <u>not</u> eat my tickets. It was <u>not</u> too cold outside. I was <u>not</u> called to Hollywood by my agent to accept a deal for a new TV sit-com based on my collected columns, starring my uncanny look-alike, Fabio. (Okay, maybe just from the neck down.)

And no, I did <u>not</u> forget. The local newspapers and radio stations made sure of that, relentlessly. And even if I'd abstained from all media, I drive by the fairgrounds regularly. The traffic jams and hordes of jaywalkers would have jogged my misfiring memory.

In the past I've been both a fair attender and a fair vendor many, many times. To the point where I am experiencing fair ennui -- extreme burnout.

There are probably others out there like me. Well, almost like me. Given the enormous local popularity of this five-day outdoor extravaganza most truants probably have the good sense not to mention their absence to any of its rabid boosters.

It is difficult to admit that one was not actually out there perspiring profusely, covered with cotton candy, and clutching a plush toy just liberated from the midway at great personal expense.

The odd thing is, once the carnies departed and this year's fair was irretrievably gone, I began suffering from PFS (post-fair syndrome). And while PFS is not a genetic condition, it may be jean-etic. My jeans obviously miss the fresh coating of grease they got each year when I wiped my hands on them after my visit to all the food concessions.

So rather than endure withdrawal symptoms, I set about cobbling together a virtual fairground experience right here at Clear Creek Ranch. Plenty of trees and sunshine, pungent barnyard smells, and undercooked food to go around.

To make my fairytale fair as lifelike as possible, I started by driving a mile-and-a-half out to our mailbox, parking there, and walking back home in the noonday sun. My wife did not accompany me.

"You go simulate 'the parking lot experience,' dear," she said. "I'll stay here in the shade and simulate the 'dropped off at the main gate' experience."

Once home, I discovered that I wasn't completely dehydrated, and decided to stand fully-clothed in the sauna until either my eyebrows or my shirt spontaneously combusted from the heat. Again my wife declined to join in the fun, saying she was too busy with "the interactive quilt display." Actually she was laying on it. We only have the one quilt, and it's on our bed.

After the sauna I spritzed myself all over with a potent fairgrounds moisturizer homemade from stale soda pop, sugar cubes and cooking grease. Then I "bought" myself a paper cup loaded with soft drink-coated ice cubes and strolled over to visit the fine canned goods display in our pantry.

Most of my time was spent in the Pointless Produce Preservation section, where we keep things we harvest and can every year but never quite get around to eating. It is fascinating how the color of canned goods changes as years go by. The gray tomato-like entities won Best of Show.

Then, before I simulated a carnival ride experience by spinning around until I'm dizzy and nauseated, it was time to eat. Fair food is finger food! That is, food stuck to all your fingers, dripping down your forearms and up past the elbows.

Undercooked tofu hotdogs smeared with coagulated condiments sounded good to me -- as long as they were properly prepared. You've got to drop them on the ground a few times and sort of rinse off the big foreign chunks with whatever you are drinking. My wife quickly informed me that she had just begun a 24-hour fast.

Add a sticky fly-blown picnic bench in full sun and some overpowering barnyard aroma. I placed a sack of manure upwind, on top of a big wad of crumpled dollar bills (representing my usual fair time fiscal irresponsibility), and fired it up until it was smoldering vigorously. To complete the fairground ambience I simulated a realistic crowd by surrounding myself with assorted lifesize cutouts from TV's America's Most Wanted, Baywatch/Weightwatchers, and a PBS jailhouse tattoo documentary. My wife just doesn't know what she's missing.

Or, then again, maybe she does.

140

A More Or Les Miserable Day

It was the best of days, it was the worst of days -- it was a Dickens of a day, and it was supposed to be my day off. We had nothing planned until evening -- a special dinner in town at a restaurant where reservations were hard to come by. Our reward for living so simply out in the country. I was whittling on a stick near the fireplace, or some such rustic thing, when my wife approached me.

"The bathtub is going to overflow," she said.

"Perhaps you should turn the water off, dear."

"But the water isn't on, dear."

If our plumbing system was a coronary system it badly needed a bypass. Everything was clogged. In the past I'd fixed similar problems by opening a clean-out valve and jiggling around with an old eight-foot wire "snake." No big deal. Country folks are self-reliant. I inched my way into the tight crawl space and loosened the valve cover, realizing a second too late that there must be a lot of pressure in the pipes to have filled the bathtub. The cover popped off and twenty gallons of "water" gushed out before I could get out of the way. Through the floor from the bathroom above my head, I heard my wife's cheerful voice, "The water's going down, dear."

The little snake didn't work its magic, so I half-heartedly rinsed off and headed for the rental yard in town. Because of my ripe condition I took my old junker truck, the one I'd recently used to pick up a load of manure for the garden. I'd put off unloading the manure and it was steaming pungently inside the camper shell and forward into the cab (for which there was no back window).

The Rental Yard Guy had probably seen do-it-yourself homeowners in worse shape before, so he didn't bat an eye at my appearance. I did notice that no one stood near me at the counter, and the Rental Yard Guy, whose name was Victor, nonchalantly flipped on an industrial strength fan behind him that blew everything on the counter toward me, and he began to breathe out of the corner of his mouth like a swimmer. Hugo, the Rental Yard Guy's assistant, lacked subtlety, appearing as he did, wearing a gas mask and carrying the "giant fifty-foot snake" I had rented.

"I'll be back," I said.

"We'll hold our breath."

Luckily (I thought) the problem was in a newer part of the system. I'd wisely insisted on an easy access clean-out when the contractor laid out the plans. I fed the monster snake into the pipe while standing almost comfortably, in the drizzling rain. The snake sailed through the pipes and it wasn't until it began tapping me on the back that I realized the snake had gone up through the roof vent instead of down toward the septic tank. The clean-out valve had been installed backwards.

An extra step, but surmountable, even in the now-pouring rain. I dug out the pipe, cut it, cleaned out the problem with the snake, returned it to the rental yard (world's record for fastest check-in), and bought some ABS pipe fixtures. ABS is a type of plumbing pipe. The letters stand for "Atrocious Black Stuff," which is an irremovable solvent I got on my hands and clothes as I glued the pipes together under the impromptu tarp lean-to I erected to protect the pipes from the downpour.

As the last pipe fitting dried, the tarp gave way under the weight of trapped rainwater and a torrent of rust and dirt from our picturesque metal roof drenched me.

I staggered dripping into the house and attempted a cheerful "Hi honey, I'm home" just as the electricity went out. At Clear Creek Ranch power outages mean no lights, no pump, no water.

Who knew how long before power was restored. Our dinner reservations were in an hour.

My wife, bless her, refused to go alone. She quickly called, and irretrievably cancelled our reservations. As she hung up the phone, the lights flickered on.

"You could use a good soak, dear," my wife said. "I mean a bath." She gets extra points for not holding her nose.

"I think I deserve one," I piped. "I'm feeling drained."

Off the Deep End

The seasonal rains turn Clear Creek into a raging rivulet for about two months each year. The pond fills and the bullfrogs emerge. (From where exactly -- did they drop from the sky along with the rain?) Over the next few weeks the muddy waters clear and migrating ducks paddle on its placid surface, suddenly plunging their heads beneath to snack at the underwater salad bar, their feathered bottoms bobbing skyward.

As I watch, a seasonal longing begins to overpower me. And no, my longing involves no urge to grab a shotgun and "blast those quacking suckers." I envy them, floating peacefully on the pond I created. Well, the Pond Guy actually created it with a bulldozer and a lot of my money, but I like to forget that part of it.

About this time I sigh and say, "I think I'll build a boat."

And my wife says, "Ahoy, matey, isn't that reality I see sinking off the starboard poopdeck?"

Sometimes here in our rural mountain home there isn't much separation between scenic beauty and a cynic beauty, especially when she knows me so well.

But I possess the pioneer spirit. I didn't move "back to the land" because I was a quitter. I was determined to build a seaworthy vessel at any cost, as long as there was no cash involved.

In my quest I partially retraced the evolution of the boat itself. Having many books on self-sufficiency on the rickety shelves of the Clear Creek Ranch library, I soon found my direction -- several directions, really.

"Grab your adze and go chopping for a log," one pamphlet urged. A hollowed log -- a dugout canoe -- seemed like the perfect primitive water transport for a rustic mountain person such as I.

The problem was chopping myself a new adze-hole that was big enough to sit in without cutting through the other side of the log. After several tries and such words of spousal encouragement as, "Nice bunch of firewood you've got there," I was ready for a change. But I wasn't discouraged. If anything, my zeal was re-kindled.

Animalskin-covered frames were another early boat form. But, as my wife was quick to point out, all the available animal skins at Clear Creek Ranch were still holding their original animals together. I cast about for a suitable synthetic alternative.

I needed look no farther than my closet where rack upon rack of the once plentiful, but now nearly-extinct turtlenecked velour still abounds. There are no PBS specials showing herds of migrating velour fording rivers, and for good reason, something to do with excessive absorbency.

Moving forward to 20th century boatbuilding techniques, I tried to utilize some large warped plywood scraps that had been "ageing" in the garage for a few years.

I selected a simple, flat-bottomed skiff design and was hard at work when my wife came out, apparently to discuss the dining plans for my bon voyage party.

"It's past noon. Do you want launch?" she asked.

"Not yacht," I replied.

I stood back, waiting for sighs of admiration at the shallow boxy rectangle I'd constructed.

"What do you think?" I asked.

"Add a few horizontal pieces and it would make a nice bookcase for all those 'how-to' books of yours," she said.

Well, her comments held no water with me, and I hauled my skiff down to the pond to test its seaworthiness. I gently coaxed its nose into the water and gave it a little shove. Then I stood back and watched it settle quickly to the bottom.

As soon as it dries out, I'll be fitting it with shelves.

I Got Rhizome
Who Could Ask For Anything More?

Cattails, my eclectic garden reference library tells me, are known as bulrushes in Britain. The word bulrush sounds vaguely biblical: Egypt, papyrus, Moses during his early upwardly mobile phase as a diapered yachtsman on the Nile.

I could certainly use his sort of services to help part the dense growth that has resulted from six tiny cattail sprouts I planted around our pond a few years ago.

It takes a sharp machete, a strong arm, and a good sense of direction to make it to the water's edge now. The plants tower overhead, blocking the sun. Things squish and crunch underfoot. Every inch of vegetation is teeming with snakes and bloodthirsty insects.

When I lost my way and spent a night thrashing about in the general direction of the calls from the search and rescue team, I decided something had to be done.

I couldn't use the usual poisons without killing everything in the pond. So I tried to eradicate the cattails, laboriously pulling them up by the roots, only to have them all return the next year.

After several futile attempts at manual herbicide, I swallowed my pride (and some kind of flying bug, I think), and called in a local expert.

"Rhizomes," my know-it-all neighbor said, nodding his shaggy head sagely (I listened closely, but didn't hear anything rattle). "You got to get every bit of that fat root out of the ground, or it'll just keep growing."

How exactly I was to accomplish this, he didn't know. But I am happy to report that after sifting several tons of pond dirt, I have permanently cleared a modest pathway almost all the way to the water's edge.

Along the way I have developed a healthy regard for the vitality of your average plant of the rhizominous-type.

One morning not long ago I awoke to find a huge mound of rhizome-like entities heaped on my front porch.

"They're not satisfied controlling the pond," I screamed. "Now the rogues want to force their way inside!"

A note was pinned to one of them. At least it wasn't hieroglyphics printed on papyrus. It seemed to be English and identified them as iris plants, as in bearded iris -- beautiful flowers, usually blooming in the springtime.

We had an empty flowerbed for them, and they are so pretty I wouldn't care if, over time, they spread like weeds. Of course, before they could spread, they needed to get into the ground, and that would entail several hours of backbreaking labor.

And they were rhizomes. Who knew what they were capable of. I had a nagging question, silly really, but one that sent me rushing to my teetering reference library.

What is the plural of iris? "Irises" seemed clumsy, and a latinesque "eye-rye" sounded pretentious.   And what about the beard<u>less</u> iris, does it shave? And if so, how?

Unfortunately, whenever I dip my ladle into the wellsprings of learning I not only mix my metaphors, but I often end up on the wrong page.

The study of the iris, I read, is known as iridology. The health of the entire body is revealed by reading the subtle shades of the rods and cones. But of course, that iris is not outside in the garden, it's in your head. So many aspects of gardening are all in your head, I've found. There is even a minor science, sclerology, that scans the blood vessels of the whites of one's eyes in search of disease. But I digress.

Iris, as all you educated misters and mythes know, is the Greek goddess of the rainbow and a messenger from the other gods.

"And what other gods are those?" I asked myself, hunting for an old copy of Edith Hamilton's <u>Mythology</u> among the stacks of my cluttered reference library.

The sun was setting on my garden patch by the time I finished reading about them all. The whites of my strained eyes were covered with a fresh batch of bloodshot veins -- a sclerologist's delight, I am sure.

As darkness fell, I breathed a sigh of relief. The planting of the iris bed would have to wait until the next day. A new day . . . Eos is the goddess of dawn, isn't she? I just read that somewhere, didn't I?

Excuse me while I look that up. This will only take a minute.

Nonplussed on My Ten-Plus

I spent yesterday afternoon trying to remember if the extended warranty on my new weedwhacker includes heroic and costly Search and Rescue efforts by the Sheriff's Posse. If it does, they would need a special Shetland Pony Division to make it through all the low overhanging branches between me and civilization (such as it is here at Clear Creek Ranch).

And speaking of branches, I also wondered how to distinguish vultures from turkey buzzards. A whole bunch were perched overhead. They seemed a little disappointed. It's understandable. After three hours of cutting brush in the hot sun, I did smell like I'd been dead for a week.

The birds' problem was that I wasn't carrion. Mine was that I wasn't carrying . . . my survival kit. You know, the little pouch filled with things I usually need during an afternoon in the woods: insect repellant, band-aids, compass, splints, flares, machetes, tourniquets, grappling hooks, cutlasses, transponders, dress shields, and oxygen tents. I figure I abandoned my survival packet right after I stood on top of that ant hill my weedwhacker decapitated, and right before I did that impromptu slam-dance.

Our heavily-wooded and otherwise pristine ten acre parcel is littered with randomly-deposited packets of hand tools and farm implements abandoned during my traumatic chance-encounters with hostile members of the animal and vegetable kingdoms.

I like to think that these items are not really lost, just "cached," stowed away for future use as the pioneers used to do. I'm doing my part to ensure that America never becomes a completely cache-less society.

Anyway, as you all know, a rural roadside ditch is a lot like a middle-aged man's ear -- both are subject to rampant, unsightly, virulent growths best removed by mechanical means. Early that morning I'd plugged my own superbly virile and virulent ears and fired up the latter to clear out the former (the ditch, if you aren't following this).

As is often the case with me and repetitive manual labor, while my back and hands toiled on, my mind ranged far and wide in a completely different direction.

"Schizting" my wife calls it -- from schizophrenia, an often enviable condition that involves losing contact with reality. I, on the other hand, would prefer to have my spiritual rambles described in terms that are more psychic than psychotic.

Soon I had mentally <u>and</u> physically veered from the road, head down, deep in thought, obliterating every living piece of vegetation that didn't hold forth the btu-potential of firewood. Other than vigorously de-bugging myself occasionally, I didn't stop until the gas tank was empty.

Then I looked around to find myself in a thicket of manzanita and oak so dense I couldn't see the sky. If you haven't noticed, one gnarly manzanita tree looks pretty much like another. And they aren't terribly articulate. Just try getting good directions from one.

I had no idea where I was. But since I hadn't lacerated myself with barbed wire during my reverie, I figured I was still somewhere on the ranch. Inspecting my bug-bite-covered torso, I deduced that I had, however, crossed the inflammation superhighway.

To avoid walking in circles, I decided to mark my position with something visible. Lengths of bright orange weedwhacker line would work, so I gnawed off a piece and tied it to a tree. I would have used my knife, but only the hostile homeless ants knew where that was.

When I started to gnaw off another piece it wedged between my teeth like a thick orange piece of dental floss. An implacable plastic umbilical cord joined me to my machine, now transformed into some sort of grotesque gasoline-driven plaque-whacker. Talking was impossible, drooling was quite easy. Walking was difficult, although I did evolve a sort of tangled, strangled two-step. Death from embarrassment seemed eminent. (Last Tango Embarrassed?) I envisioned the Shetland Pony Posse arriving weeks later to discover my buzzard-picked bones still tethered thusly.

"Some 'whacky' sort of cult member with an oral hygiene fetish," the searchers would conclude. The laconic manzanita wouldn't disagree.

Fortunately the survivalist in me knew that if I headed downhill (my day was already doing that!) I would eventually hit running water, which meant civilization or my neighbor's house depending on which way I turned at the bridge.

I made it home on my second guess.

My Time In The Sun

My cats taught me all I know about solar energy. Most mornings are cool here at Clear Creek Ranch, and the cats don't like to be cold. They find a shaft of sunlight and sit in it while they practice the feline art known as the Condescending Slow-motion Eye-Blink. Soon their fur is a good ten degrees warmer than the rest of the room, they are purring comfortably, and are ready for another busy day of napping.

I've tried warming myself that way, but it never quite works. Perhaps the shaft of light isn't big enough, or I'm not furry enough, or maybe I just need a few pointers on my eye-blinking technique.

Our house has a solar water heater with four big panels up on the roof which work very well when the sun is out. Too well, actually. By 2:00 PM on a sunny day, the temperature of our solar-heated water is about the same as the surface temperature of the sun. When I draw myself an afternoon bath I'm tempted to toss in a few bits of carrot and celery and season myself to taste. Maybe change my name to Stew.

We've never seriously considered solar-generated electricity however, because of the start-up costs. Besides, the power company lines were in when we got here. Although that does make us subject to their petty whims and the vagaries of the black-out roulette they play. Our power fails (without fail) every fortnight, never at the same time of day, and often for only a few seconds. Long enough to set every VCR and digital clock in the house to blinking. I usually reset everything based on the time displayed by our battery-driven clock.

When that battery failed, I was lost, adrift in a sea of timelessness. The only other reliable timepiece at the ranch was a sand-filled three-minute egg-timer. It was going to be tedious flipping that every few minutes, and keeping track of the flip-count -- providing I knew what time it was when I started. The wrist on my flipping hand began to seize-up and ache just thinking about all that repetitive motion. And my imagined pain didn't even have a trendy name like carpal tunnel syndrome. I lost no time carping to my wife about "our" predicament.

"Perhaps, my chronologically-chronic one," she said sunnily, "the hour is at hand to install that sundial you've had stashed in the shed all these many, excuse the expression, moons."

Solar power -- why hadn't I thought of that? Well, I had. But I knew that proper placement of a sundial would require Mikey's big hand and little hand to apply mathematical principles misplaced in some high school homeroom long ago. I had to learn astronomy and develop a lot of arcane, single-use knowledge, like the exact location of "true north." I definitely had to locate an old Phoenician and persuade him to part with his astrolabe, or maybe visit an "adults only" store to purchase a sextant, then try to find the horizon among the trees and pretend to know what an "azimuth" is.

Or, as my wife pointed out, I could overcome my innate male reluctance and actually read the installation directions. They were to the point: align the gnomon parallel to the axis of the earth, adjusting its angle equal to the latitude of the site (about 39° according to my dog-earred World Atlas). Just one question, what is a gnomon? and would I gno one when I saw one?

Instead, I lugged the sundial over to a flat sunny spot and then followed this rather non-scientific regimen: I sat in the shade in my truck with the radio on. When a certain conservative talk show host signed off I rushed over and scootched the sundial around until the shadow read high noon. It's worked great ever since.

There can be several drawbacks to sundials. In overcast weather, the only answer to "What time is it?" is "Daytime." It is useless indoors, even with a klieg light shining directly on it. You can't read one accurately by flashlight in the dark. And spilling sun-block on the dial can make it unreadable for a few days. Which is about as often as I need to know what time it is, anyway.

Our cats have no use for the sundial. They sniffed it once and then gave me a few slow blinks to let me know they'd prefer a birdbath out there on the lawn.

If I'd been paying attention to our cats, they would have taught me all I need to know about time, too. From their point of view it's either time to eat, or time to sleep.

Wake me when dinner's ready.

Water and (True) Power

Tap water comes from the faucet. It fills a drinking glass, or a bath tub, or the tank behind the toilet. When I lived in the city that's all I knew. I didn't think about the mechanics of how it got to my house or where it came from. I also knew was that water was dirt cheap. It was the smallest utility bill I paid each month. So when I moved out to the country I wasn't too impressed when I found that I could get all the water I wanted from my own well "for free."

My well is located a downhill from the house near a pond, about a hundred yards away. It is rated at 30 gallons per minute, not that I have ever been in that big a hurry for 30 gallons of water. My real estate agent told me it was a fantastic well, and I took her at her word. My only previous experience with wells had been with the "wishing" variety, and I wondered how many coins and chewing gum wrappers I would find beneath the protective chicken wire cover. But my well has no quaint oaken bucket attached to a hand crank, it is a six inch pipe sticking out of the ground connected to a small electronic control panel.

The key word in the last paragraph is electronic. We have more water than we can use as long as we have electric power. Which we don't have, on average, about one day a month. According to the local power company there is this special breed of terrorist squirrels who conduct regular kamikaze-like raids on rural transformers. These bushy-tailed commandos invariably go on to their reward with a spectacular sizzling finale, but not before they knock out power to my place. Why have they singled me out? I've never espoused any anti-squirrelist sentiments. Or are these little acorn-eaters simply unwitting dupes of the power companies? Generally I don't believe these conspiracy theories, still . . .

Water: can't stay dry with it, can't bathe without it. And most importantly, occasional deposits to the water closet cannot be transferred in a timely manner to their intended place in the septic system. The ironic thing is that most of our household water shortages occur when the house itself is surrounded by water in either its liquid or solid state. Heavy winter rain and winds are hard on the old trees near my place. As their roots loosen in the soggy soil, their misguided limbs reach out to nearby power lines for support. Snow brings freezing temperatures (or is it the other way around?) and that means burst hummingbird feeders and frozen pipes.

Lucky for us, we have a year-round spring at the far end of the property. So even when we are without power, we aren't powerless. All that is required is that I fill up the five gallon cans and bring them to the house. When I realized we really did have "free" running water, I trotted down the trail to our spring, swinging a five gallon bucket in each hand. In case you didn't know, a gallon of water weighs about eight pounds. The distance to our spring is a short jaunt downhill, or an impossible struggle uphill depending on the contents of the buckets. Let's be realistic . . . when the buckets are full, I can only handle one at a time, and when I get to the house the knuckles on my "bucket hand" are a lot closer to the ground than they were before I started.

After one particularly slippery trip up our steep trail with forty pounds of water sloshing by my side, I collapsed into a chair on the porch to catch my breath. As I recovered, I gazed proudly at the container of crystal clear spring water I had brought home. I thought I saw the same proud look in my wife's eyes as she looked at the bucket.

"Can we pore that into the toilet tank for an emergency flush?" she smiled.

Half an hour's work down the drain. Greater love hath no man . . .

Drinks Courtesy of Lady Clairol

Things sure are different out in the country.

Take these tiny black specks in the bottom of my water glass, for example. When I lived in the city within easy skateboarding distance to the ocean, the specks might have been grains of sand, to consumed by the pound with any meal eaten at the beach, or tracked home by happy accident after a long day enjoying the sea breeze. Over the years we developed a small "shoreline" in our backyard from the many particles we rinsed off our persons with the garden hose.

Now that I've moved hundreds of miles away and inland, the specks have another meaning. These little irritants must have come from my drinking water's source, and that source can only be at the bottom of my own personal well.

There may be a picturesque ranch somewhere where the water well has that quaint "wishing well look:" a circular stone and mortar rim, a cutely shingled roof, and a hand crank for hauling up cool oaken bucketsful from the depths at the end of the rope. Unfortunately, that picturesque ranch is not named Clear Creek. And I am near the end of my rope on this well subject, and not feeling well at all.

It all started the day I started to take a shower and passed out from the smell -- a smell by the way that emanated not from me (that odor is garlic) but from the shower water. There I lay until the contents of our water heater was emptied and cold water began to revive me. The aroma was still intense: imagine rotten egg sandwiches with a morning-mouth chaser at the sulphur-works.

"Yube godda do subding abowb dis awful sting, dear," my nasally-pinched wife said as she handed me a fresh towel and my own olfactory-protector straight from the clothesline.

After I dried myself off and aired myself out, I tucked a jar of the vile liquid under my arm and headed to town in search of the Water Service Guy.

His burly lab assistant passed out from the smell when he unscrewed the lid to my jar. That certainly made me feel better. At least I wasn't alone.

Later that day the report came back.

"You've got hydrogen-sulfide molecules everywhere, son," the Water Service Guy said. "There is probably a colony of 'em down the well, and no doubt they are multiplying on your dip tube even as we speak. I suggest we cut yours off immediately."

My hands made an involuntarily grab into a defensive position near my groin. I didn't relax until he explained that a dip tube is not some rural euphemism for what I, and many other males, consider to be an essential body part, but is actually a semi-useless component of most water heaters.

In addition to radical amputation, another possible treatment involved the installation of a filter system. But this meant digging up buried water pipes, something I'd done once before. Whoever laid out the original network of piping here at the ranch must have used a butterfly's peripatetic flight plan as a guide. When I finally unearthed them all, I found pipes that forked and crossed and stubbed-out endlessly for no apparent reason.

Since both the removal and installation procedures would involve the Plumbing Guy, and since we already had a second mortgage on Clear Creek Ranch, I opted to try a less radical treatment first. The Water Service Guy suggested pouring a gallon of bleach down the well and letting it sit overnight.

"That should kill most of those pesky molecules," he said confidently.

It certainly killed our morning beverage when I perked it using a freshly drawn coffeepot full of barely diluted bleach. As my wife gagged, I tried to distract her by pointing out that "the smell" was gone. Nothing could live in our water now.

I mentioned that I'd seen TV ads for "clear beer" but this was the first time I'd ever had "clear coffee" -- not decaf, but caffeine-light.

"Yes, let's look on the bright side," my wife said. "Now you can finally quit worrying whether Juan Valdez washed his hands before he picked our coffee beans."

So far, the bleach treatment seems to have worked its magic and the smell remains gone. There were other pluses too, as the bleach worked its way through our water system. After one shampoo my thinning hair became more fashionably blonde than grey. And the little mold spots that were beginning to form on the bottom edge of the shower curtain suddenly disappeared.

Best of all, I got to leave my dip tube intact.

Zen And The Art
Of Whirligig Maintenance

Part of the training of Zen Buddhist monks involves the contemplation of koans -- seemingly paradoxical statements. "What is the sound of one hand clapping?" for example. The objective is a sudden, intuitive enlightenment on the part of the neophyte. An ice cream koan is sometimes given as a reward, but not if it will spoil the monklet's dinner.

While I am not a consistent student of this ancient philosophy (I fall into the "now and zen" category), I do know something about the sound of one-half of a propeller slapping. It happens all the time on the windward side of our house, and can mean only one thing -- it is the end of the whirl for another one of my whirligigs.

I've got dozens of these homemade wind toys mounted to every square inch of deck railings and fence posts here at Clear Creek Ranch. Folk art, naive art. Lumber scraps in whimsical shapes that creak and clatter in the breeze.

Surely you've seen a whirligig, perhaps you even have one. Wooden birds, their "wings" spinning with improbable speed. Eternally optimistic jockeys on horseback endlessly circling a racetrack without finish line. Rock stars flailing "air guitars." Native Americans paddling over rapids in "air canoes."

If I could harness the energy generated by their whirling blades it would just about pay for the electricity expended by my power tools in creating them. But since I can barely put the chain back on the bar of my chainsaw when it comes loose, the prospects are slim that I will successfully rig an electronic interface between a deep cycle storage battery and my little-wooden-man-furiously-milking-a-placid-wooden-cow wind toy.

My wife attached a little engraved plaque on that one so that visitors would know what it was. An early observer had been offended, assuming that it depicted something obscene going on between an extraterrestrial and an endangered species. Not a bad theme for a wind toy now that I think of it, but certainly not one I had intended.

Let's just say that my wood carving technique leans toward the abstract. Which may be the result of my personal artistic vision, although it could be due to the bulky bandages I acquire on most of my fingers during a typical carving session. My wife insists I can turn any activity into a blood sport.

As a result of such strong moral support here at home, many of my primal whirligigs served as kindling for our woodstove. Some because they flew apart in high winds, others because they blew apart due to imbalance in the propellers, but most because I was trying to "destroy the evidence." Some of the better, but un-wind-worthy ones did make it inside the ranch house where they catch dust rather than breezes.

During those early frustrating days I was tempted to attempt some simpler wind devices: wind chimes, for example. True, chimes have moving parts, but those parts are designed to bang together forming a delightfully delicate cacophony of music-like sound. My wife liked the idea.

And if one is pleasant, how pleasurable would forty be? For that is the number of wind chimes that soon hung under the eaves near our dining room window. Unable to admit our error, we wore earmuffs that summer during mealtimes. Until a high wind mercifully snarled them together and I had to cut them down (only nicked two fingers that time). They lie entwined forever (if I have my way) in an unmarked box buried deep in the stacks of the far corner of the shed.

And now that every exterior horizontal surface within reach is covered with brightly-colored whirligigs, and the interior surfaces are strewn with gee-gaws, there is only one way to go . . . up. Up on the roof we have over ninety feet of unobstructed ridge line. And I just got a book of weathervane patterns in the mail. It won't be long now before I have a few dozen more opinions on which way the wind is blowing.

What Blight Through Yonder Window?

Clear Creek Ranch is situated such that we don't worry much about the neighbors secretly peeping into the bunkhouse windows at night. If they want to gawk, they'd have to deal with the steep, uneven terrain, and crash through several acres of chaparral and poison oak first.

This fact coupled with the obvious energy inefficiency of (me) closing drapes every evening and opening them every morning is why our ranch house windows remain relatively unadorned. And that is a lot of un-adornment, since about 80% of the wall space on three sides of the house are nothing but massive slabs of glass.

To be totally honest, we had to put something on the outside of these windows. Our native bird population is either kamikazically suicidal or in dire need of a trip to the optometrist. An inordinate number of birds have taken great pains to fly into our great panes.

Using brightly-colored surveyor's tape, we strung a huge X across each window. This makes the house look either like it is condemned, or under perpetual construction, but my wife insists the ribbons give the place a festive air.

The fluttering Xs are supposed to warn the birds about the glass. The system works moderately well. Birds still crash land, but none of them has ever hit the ribbons.

Whatever optical disillusionment the windows create for our feathered friends is offset by the enhancement of my own personal vision. When the afternoon light is right, I can see the neutrinos landing in our orchard.

For those of you who were absent that day in high school physics class, a neutrino is an uncharged subatomic particle associated with either electrons or muons (who can keep track!). Conventional wisdom may say that neutrinos are invisible, but I know what I'm seeing through my own windows.

My wife tried to explain it all away, calling it eye fatigue, dementia caused by that second glass of wine with dinner, or simply light refracted off the heavy layer of dust and diagonal cobwebs that festoon the exterior of everything around here.

I held out for as long as I could, claiming to be a misunderstood and persecuted pioneer in the Gaze Rights Movement, but secretly I knew she was right. The neutrinos just weren't there if I stood outside on the deck looking for them. They were only visible through the glass. There was, I knew, only one thing left to do -- wash the windows. Acres of windows.

I've watched storefront window washers at work. They suds up everything and then wield their squeegee like a rapier, and with a few swordfighter-like moves (giving new meaning to dual-paned/duel-pained glass) produce a thing of beauty -- a least until that first greasy forehead presses up against it.

The windows here at Clear Creek Ranch often need stone cutting tools to chip the surface free of debris. I've tried powerblasting them with the garden hose (be sure to close <u>all</u> the windows before you try this) only to discover our walls have more and bigger leaks than the average Senate subcommittee.

Razorblades can be used to remove some stubborn lumps, but speaking from sad experience, they can also scratch the glass. As can a not-quite-clean rag. When my wife complained of a few streaks on one of my finished masterpieces, I discovered the marks were permanent. (Cleaning tip: sandpaper is not the answer here, unless you are going for that opaque look).

So, while privacy is not an issue here at the Ranch, covering up one's mistakes is. We called in a New Age organic window-covering specialist. All her fabrics are made from vegetable fibers, mostly grains: oats, barley, wheat, etc. I call her the cereal drapist. My wife thinks I'm fighting this whole decorating idea, but I'm not. I've taken a wheat and see attitude.

My wife just warned me, saying it's curtains for me if I write one more corny pun that goes against the grain.

Hay, I can see her point of view. But not through our windows.

A Witness Protection Program?

The human spirit is never satisfied, is it? I work from home, right here at Clear Creek Ranch, surrounded by the ones I love, fresh air, a beautiful view, and virtual silence. No boss, just a stack of notes and deadlines. I tap words into my computer, then modem, fax, or mail off the results, and miraculously, paychecks (tiny ones, I grant you) roll in.

"They," the ones who pay me, don't even know what I look like. Oh sure, they have that publicity photo I sent them, the one where my hair is combed and I'm wearing a coat and tie. My smiling head may even head this column as you read it. But I don't dress that way when I write.

My usual uniform is a ratty bathrobe and slippers. Like the ones I'm wearing right now. It's hard to get motivated and "dress for success" in a worsted three-piece, rep tie and wingtips each morning when I know all I'm facing is a forty-five second commute from the kitchen coffee pot to my sparsely appointed office-like crawl space over the garage.

When I worked at a "real" job in the city, I would have envied me. Even now, sometimes I envy me. But then something disturbing happens, like it did the other day when I went into the bank. All those financial types were wearing jeans and shortsleeved shirts instead of their usual uniforms: suits and dresses. It was "Dress Down Day" for the employees. Which is fine with me. They were still better dressed than most of the customers -- than me, for sure. And the break in routine probably lifted morale.

Or may have lowered it. I wore a uniform to parochial school, except on certain days when the nuns let us wear whatever we wanted. It took about five times as long to dress on those days. Here was a chance to make a statement, to be an individual, to stand out from the crowd.

I arrived at school in all my blinding sartorial splendor only to discover I was wearing a slight variation of what every other guy my age was wearing, i.e. what was "cool" that week, i.e. another kind of uniform. The kids who stuck out were the ones who forgot it was Dress Down Day and wore their regular uniforms.

So if I'm supposed to wear a suit and tie to dress up and old jeans and a tee-shirt to dress down, what am I supposed to wear on normal days? Where does totally unclothed come in? Don't tell me naked isn't normal. Well, maybe not at the bank, but seated here at my computer in the summertime it could be. Although I probably won't opt for that. But if I did, I'd rather be nude than naked. Nude sounds much classier, don't you think? There is an air of legitimacy to it -- artist's models pose nude, whereas Playboy centerfolds are naked. And while Playboy centerfolds can be impressive, working at home, there is no one to impress either by dressing up or down.

Usually.

The other morning I was definitely dressed down, even by my low standards. My uncombed hair was twisted and teased into improbable shapes by the malicious coif pixies that lurk in my bedroom, my chin whiskers were enjoying their second consecutive day away from the razor, I hadn't yet brushed my teeth, and my coffee-stained "coat of many colors" bathrobe, beltless in this decade, was flapping open to reveal my relatively fresh, but less than sterling underwear.

I was up in my office when I heard the car pull up. Living out where we do, we don't have many people "drop in" unexpectedly, except maybe the UPS guy or a station wagon full of Jehovah's Witnesses. I looked out the window. It wasn't the UPS guy.

Assorted "dressed up" Witnesses were tumbling out of the car like so many circus clowns. One was already knocking on the door and yelling, "yoohoo." Everyone was smiling and peppy. And, I knew from experience, very persistent. I could hide as long as I wanted, but they weren't leaving until they talked to me. I stapled my robe shut with the electric staple gun, but it got stuck and just hung there halfway down my robe. I unplugged it, and went downstairs, careful not to trip on the dangling cord.

The boss Witness chatted with me as if this were the highlight of her day. I accepted some literature, and they were off to my neighbor's house, where I hope he was nice to them. Door to door evangelism has got to be a tough career choice.

I wonder what they thought of my staple gun? Sometimes I think they show up just to witness my choice of attire for the day. Surely Jehovah will figure that alone is penance enough to ensure their direct entry into heaven. I'm glad I could help.

My State of the Ranch Address

In preparation for my annual State of the Ranch address, I visited our orchard for the first time in months. Things were a little parched up there. Apparently the expensive automated drip irrigation system I installed last year hasn't been working at all. In my speech I plan to put a positive spin on it -- water consumption is down!

Wizened would be an accurate but unattractive way to describe our bumper crop of shrivelled nectarines and peaches. How about this: a trendy new form -- fruit leathers. Drying the fruit right there on the trees saved on labor costs, too. Leaving the pits in provides an added snack time challenge and should boost revenues for local dental health practitioners.

Elsewhere on the food production front: most of the garden lies fallow this season, sprouting an arid bumper crop of star thistle and anemic johnny-jump-ups. I had all the best intentions last April, but a sudden hailstorm coupled with a rototiller that refused to function on year-old shellacky gasoline did me in. Clearly a case of hail-fallow-well meant. By the time I retooled, refueled, and was ready to till, the weeds had too much of a head start. Sew it is "till weed meet again next year" in the garden.

"Eating our weedies" may be on the menu this winter when food reserves run low, even though abundant harvests are anticipated in our substantial marjoram, lavender, tansy, and borage sectors. Unfortunately no funds were ever appropriated toward researching what, if any, purpose these herbs serve in sustaining life -- human or otherwise.

On the supply side: this winter's firewood is already neatly stacked in rows four feet high and thirty-two feet long, buttressed at regular intervals by cross stacked cribbing.

It is located downhill from here on an almost level piece of land easily viewed through our kitchen window with moderately-powered binoculars. The exact distance from woodpile to woodstove is not known, although from personal experience it appears to be about two steps this side of a massive coronary, an imprecise measurement to be sure.

Attempts to supplement our usual fuel supply with tree branches trimmed where they overhang the ranchhouse roof have been a "crashing" disappointment. Projected gains in free firewood were more than offset by losses in branch-shattered dual-pane windows and a badly mangled TV antenna. None of our many fogged-up dual-panes were among those broken -- a fact that pains me to this day.

Transportation matters continue unchanged. Here at Clear Creek Ranch we remain in a boring vehicular rut, so to speak. Our vehicles are always driven off-center, out of some of the deeper ranch road ruts. These ruts (or seasonal streams) provide our first line of defense against unannounced visitors such as incoming hordes of Jehovah's Witnesses. Their middle of the road stationwagons generally high-center out near the front gate, giving us plenty of time to draw the blinds and/or get dressed, depending on our mood.

An added note on our attire out here at the ranch. While we have no formal dress code, a defacto uniform color of the day has been declared. Based on my inability to properly separate certain colors on laundry day, 95% of the ranch wardrobe offers us two choices: dusty rose (from my infamous cheap red socks feat), or taupe (from the "I can't believe new blue jeans still run when they're washed" debacle).

Finally on the economic front: we are working to reclassify Clear Creek Ranch as tribal land so we can tap into the burgeoning Indian slot machine casino market. Ours seems to be the only foothill community without at least one. The Ranch attorney, however, continues to have reservations.

While I admit none of my known ancestors are Native Americans, many were born on this continent and are native Americans. A few were even from Indiana, where my tribe flourished for generations before wandering westward.

But whatever state the Drummond clan was in, I doubt they ever before subsisted peacefully in harmony with nature on exotic fruit leathers while clad in distinctive clothing of muted, monochromatic tones.

Yet another Clear Creek Ranch first! (I'll pause here for the applause to die down).

Pond Memories

The summer I was five, my grandpa promised to take me on my first fishing trip. For several days preceding the actual event, as we did our chores around his farm, we, or rather I, talked excitedly about nothing else.

In the barn he managed to put together all the basic ingredients on a cluttered workbench covered in drifts of hay dust. A thin bamboo cane, a some fish line, a piece of cork, a lug nut sinker, and from an old quart jar, a fish hook.

"What about bait?" I demanded.

Although I'd never actually gone fishing, I considered myself to be an expert -- I watched cartoons. You have to sit a worm on the hook so the fish will want to eat him. Then at the last second the worm, who has eyebrows and a rather startled look on his face, scampers back up the fish line to safety, but it is too late for the open-mouthed fish charging toward him. The fish bites the hook, gets an X on each eye, and you throw him in a frying pan.

Grandpa seemed to understand the process now, and promised we would dig up some worms "first thing in the morning." He gave me an old, thin red Prince Albert tobacco can to hold them. I had to remind him about the frying pan part too. But then what could he and grandma know -- they didn't have a television, just a radio the size of our refrigerator back home.

It was a humid August night, the sky alive with lightning bugs and lightning. With each flash I saw my new fishing pole, carefully propped in the corner. The thunderstorm slapped warm, fat raindrops against the windowpane until I fell asleep.

It's hard to know when "first thing in the morning" is when you are five. The world pretty much stops when you go to sleep and starts again when you wake up.

The roosters were crowing when I got up in the dark and dressed myself. I grabbed my new fishing pole and worm can, and stepped into the hallway. The house was quiet and shadowy. I went into the kitchen and found a frying pan large enough for me to sit in. Then I waited in the hall.

It took forever before grandpa's form appeared in the gloom. He hitched up his overalls as he gently shut the bedroom door. He struck a match and sucked the flame down into the bowl of his briar pipe until the tobacco glowed.

"So, are we going now?" I asked as he walked past me.

He seemed startled and switched on the light. He truly hadn't seen me in the shadows. As he gave me and my gear the once-over, his smoke-hallowed face broke into a grin.

"Think that pan's big enough?" he asked in his soft Missouri accent.

I assured him I had high expectations.

As the indifferent cows watched, he turned over a few shovelfuls of dirt just downhill from the outhouse. In minutes I'd filled my worm can and we were on our way.

His cousin's place was only a few farms down the road. The sun was rising as we headed beyond the barn to a circular pond rimmed in sedgegrass and stocked with catfish. I had a heck of a time trying to get my worm to cooperate and sit on the hook the way I knew it should. It kept sliding off and trying to slither away.

Finally grandpa showed me his way of getting a worm to stay on the hook, which was more effective, but seemed to take some of the life out of the little guy. He left me alone to "drown a few worms" while he talked in a low voice with his cousin.

Grandpa's cousin looked like him, only bigger. They stood in the shade, folded their arms, and smoked. I pretended not to hear when grandpa told him about finding me in the hallway that morning. I squinted a little and cut my eyes their way and saw them smiling.

I got a bite! It took a while, but I yanked the fish out of the water where it lay flopping on the bank. I was disappointed to see that a catfish didn't look anything like it did in cartoons. Its face wasn't cute and kitten-like, but closer to a grumpy Edward G. Robinson with Fu Manchu moustaches. No Xs on its eyes, either.

I didn't cook the fish there, grandma did that hours later at home for lunch. By then grandpa had "done the dirty work" and cleaned the fish, or so he said. How could fish be dirty, I wondered, when they live in the water?

And my cooked fish didn't even look like a fish anymore. It certainly didn't get up and dance around like the cartoon fish did. It just laid there like any other boring piece of meat. What a gyp!

But that day was long ago. I have my own pond now, here at Clear Creek Ranch. Filled mostly with frogs and turtles, but who knows, a catfish or two might be lurking near the bottom.

I don't fish the pond much, and I haven't taken any five-year-olds fishing -- although I am sure my workshop has all the ingredients I will need to rig up some sort of impromptu fishing pole if the time comes.

I enjoy sitting on its grassy banks. And sometimes when the shadows are right I imagine I see grandpa, gone a long time now, over there in the shade: straw hat, overalls, pipe in hand, that big approving smile on his face.

Over forty years have passed since my day with him. And you know, while many things haven't turned out as I hoped they would, I still have great expectations.

To order additional copies of this book, please send check or money order payable to Clear Creek Features in the amount of $12.95 per book, plus $1.50 postage for the first book, and 50¢ extra for each additional book. CA residents please add 7¼% sales tax.

Clear Creek Features
Box 35
Rough & Ready CA 95975